PUBLIC WORKS CONTRA
CIVIL ENGINEERING WORKS
BY THE EMPLOYER

EXPLAINED

PUBLIC WORKS CONTRACT FOR CIVIL ENGINEERING WORKS DESIGNED BY THE EMPLOYER

EXPLAINED

By

James Howley
&
Martin Lang

CLARUS PRESS

Published by
Clarus Press Ltd,
Griffith Campus,
South Circular Road,
Dublin 8.

Typeset by
Compuscript Ltd,
Shannon Industrial Estate,
Shannon,
Co. Clare.

Printed by
Eprint Ltd,
Coolmine Industrial Estate,
Dublin 15.

Front Cover Photography
Aerial photo of Dublin City Centre
Gerry O'Leary © www.gerryoleary.com

ISBN
978-1-905536-19-1

A CIP catalogue record for this book is available from the British Library.

€38·25

Disclaimer
Whilst every effort has been made to ensure that the contents of this book are
accurate, neither the publisher, editor or contributors can accept responsibility for
any errors or omissions or loss occasioned to any person acting or refraining from
acting as result of any material in this publication.

ABOUT THE AUTHORS

James Howley MSc, Dip Arb, Dip Proj Mgmt, MRICS, ASCS, FCIOB, FCIArb., Chartered Arbitrator, Chartered Surveyor, Accredited Adjudicator, CIArb Accredited Mediator has over 30 years experience in the construction industry. In addition to building and civil engineering contractors, he has worked with professional consultancy practices. His experience includes large-scale building and civil engineering projects, including utilities, rail, roads, oil and power generating projects in Ireland, the UK and mainland Europe. He holds an MSc in Construction Law and Arbitration from Kings College, London and has completed formal training in arbitration, adjudication and mediation. He is currently working in private practice as a Construction Contracts Consultant, Arbitrator, Conciliator and Adjudicator.

Martin Lang MCIArb, CIArb Accredited Mediator has been involved in the construction industry at senior management level for the last 35 years. He began his career as an estimator and trained as a Quantity Surveyor in Dublin. He went on to be a Contracts Manager and Contracts Director with some of Irelands leading Civil Engineering and Construction Companies. He has had an extensive career in Project Management in the United Kingdom, Spain, Portugal, the Middle East and West Africa. He joined the Construction Industry Federation in 1995 as an Executive Officer where he is now Head of Contracts. Martin has dealt with over 200 construction mediations and conciliations.

PREFACE

Public sector construction contributes approximately €8 billion annually to the Irish construction industry. Construction projects, as a result of their inherent nature, can be subject to cost and time overruns. With such a large financial outlay and exposure to cost and time overruns, the government require more price and time certainties on public construction projects. In May 2004, the government commissioned the production of the Public Works Contracts to replace the GDLA and IEI Standard Forms of Contracts.

A new suite of construction contracts for use on Public Works contracts was published in February 2007. All public works construction projects will be carried out under these forms of contracts. This book comments on the Public Works Contract for Civil Engineering Works Designed by the Employer for use on contracts greater than €5 million. The new suite of contracts also comprise:

- Contracts greater than €5 million
  - Public Works Contract for Building Works Designed by the Employer
  - Public Works Contract for Building Works Designed by the Contractor
  - Public Works Contract for Civil Engineering Works Designed by the Contractor
- Contracts less than €5 million
  - Public Works Contract for Minor Civil Engineering and Building Works designed by the Employer
- Contracts less than €500,000.00
  - Short Form of Public Works Contract for Building and Civil Engineering Works.

The new Public Works Contracts set out strict criteria for the award of extensions of time to the project and increases to the contract sum. The contracts introduce "condition precedent" and time bar clauses whereby a contractor's claims has to be notified and submitted within a specified time period if the claims are to succeed. This new criteria introduces a new environment under which contractors must carry out business.

This book is set out with the Articles of Agreement, followed in a clause by clause format, followed by PV1, PV2 and the Schedule to the contract with an explanation on each clause as it occurs.

CONTENTS

INTRODUCTION

PUBLIC WORKS CONTRACTS

New Public Works Contracts

It is the intention of this book to explain each contract clause in a clear and easy to understand manner to allow the reader to develop an insight into how these contracts will operate. This book also includes sample documents including notices and letters which will add to the readers' understanding of the strict and critical administrative procedures demanded by these contracts.

The government required more price certainty on public contracts. To achieve this, in May 2004, the Government commissioned the production of the new Public Works Contracts. These contracts facilitate the transfer of more risks to contractors.

The Government drafting body adopted elements of risk transfer not only from traditional contracts – GDLA and IEI – but also from contracts like FIDIC, JCT, British Property Federation, Management Contracts, NEC and international power and oil projects.

The result is a suite of contracts that allows employers to transfer a far greater level of risk to contractors. The suite of new contracts are:

- PUBLIC WORKS CONTRACT FOR CIVIL ENGINEERING WORKS DESIGNED BY THE EMPLOYER issued 15th August 2007.

- PUBLIC WORKS CONTRACT FOR CIVIL ENGINEERING WORKS DESIGNED BY THE CONTRACTOR.

- PUBLIC WORKS CONTRACT FOR BUILDING WORKS DESIGNED BY THE EMPLOYER.

- PUBLIC WORKS CONTRACT FOR BUILDING WORKS DESIGNED BY THE CONTRACTOR.

- PUBLIC WORKS CONTRACT FOR MINOR CIVIL ENGINEERING AND BUILDING WORKS DESIGNED BY THE EMPLOYER (recommended for works under €5m).

- SHORT FORM OF PUBLIC WORKS CONTRACT FOR BUILDING AND CIVIL ENGINEERING WORKS (recommended for works under €500,000)

The contracts themselves have the advantage of being laid out in a clear and logical format and in general contain, in addition to the Articles of Agreement and sections dealing with Price Variations and the Schedule, 13 conditions set out using the following headings:

1. The Contract

2. The Law

3. Loss Damage and Injury (Insurances)

4. Management

5. Contractors Personnel

6. Property

7. The Site

8. Quality Testing and Defects

9. Time and Completion

10. Claims and Adjustments

11. Payment

12. Termination

13. Disputes.

It should be noted by current practitioners and students more familiar with GDLA or IEI forms of contracts that certain fundamental changes in how construction contracts are operated will occur as a result of the introduction of these contracts. In this regard, areas of particular importance are dealt with in clauses 4, 9, 10, 11 and 13. Together with these new clauses new terminology has been introduced and terms like "programme contingencies", "thresholds", "daily delay costs", "employer's representative" and "change orders" are but to name a few. These are dealt with in particular detail in the definitions to the contract and in the commentary sections.

In addition to additional risks being transferred to contractors, the contractor's recovery of costs and time have also been set to contractual conditions that are "condition precedent". This means that the contract criteria must be complied with by the contractor within set time periods if the contractor is to succeed in recovery of entitlements. In line with developments in the international construction markets and other jurisdictions "Time-Bar" clauses have also been introduced. Contractor's claims can fail, if the time-scales for the provision of initial notices of claims and the provision of full details of claims are not provided within the timescales dictated within the contract.

The new contracts are rigid, structured and follow a set format. The format is the same for building and civil engineering works for both employer's design projects and contractor design projects.

With the introduction of new Public Works Contracts not only will the contractor have to price the risks transferred to him but he will also have to price within his tender the costs of delays that may occur. These tendered costs will be taken into account by the employer when assessing tender submissions.

Contracts will not be awarded on the basis of the lowest tender. The criteria for awarding contracts will be the Most Economically Advantageous Tender (MEAT). Therefore a good deal of thought has to go into the preparation of tenders.

The new Public Works Contracts were first published on 19th February 2007. These contracts are now the norm for all public works contracts.

Contractors have to adapt not just to the new tendering requirements but also to the supervisory and administration requirements of the Public Works Contracts.

How to Use this Book

This book reproduces the Public Works Contract for Civil Engineering Works Designed by the Employer issued 15th August 2007. The book is set out in a clause by clause basis following the same format as set out in the form of contract. The commentaries on clauses of particular interest are contained in the highlighted print, giving practical explanations on the intent of the contract.

Second in a Series

Readers should note that this book is the second of a series of books by the same authors dealing with the new Public Works Contracts. Other titles in this series will deal with the remaining forms of public works contracts and related documents.

AGREEMENT

THIS AGREEMENT is made on ....BETWEEN

....(the **Employer**)

AND...

whose registered office/principal place of business is at ....(the **Contractor**).

BACKGROUND

The Employer has accepted the Contractor's tender to complete the Works, which consist, in general, of

....

THE EMPLOYER AND THE CONTRACTOR AGREE as follows:

Article 1   The Contractor shall execute and complete the Works subject to and in accordance with the Contract and shall comply with its other obligations in the Contract.

Article 2   The Employer shall pay the Contractor the Contract Sum subject to and in accordance with the Contract and shall comply with its other obligations in the Contract.

Article 3   The initial Contract Sum including VAT is ....

....(*insert in words*)

(€...). The initial Contract Sum is a lump sum and shall only be adjusted when the Contract says so.

Article 4   The Contractor has satisfied itself before entering into the Contract of all the circumstances that may affect the cost of executing and completing the Works and of the correctness and sufficiency of the Contract Sum to cover the cost of performing the Contract. The Contractor has included in the initial Contract Sum allowances for all risks, customs, policies, practices, and other circumstances that may affect its performance of the Contract, whether they could or could not have been foreseen, except for events for which the Contract provides for adjustment of the initial Contract Sum.

Article 5   The Contract consists of the following documents:

- this Agreement
- the Letter of Acceptance and any post-tender clarifications listed in it
- the attached Conditions and completed Schedule
- the Works Requirements, completed Pricing Document, and Works Proposals identified in the attached Schedule

Article 6   The Contract takes effect from the Contract Date.

The Employer

Given under the Employer's seal

....   affix Employer's seal

....
(*signatures of persons authorised to authenticate the seal*)

OR **Signed** on behalf of the Employer

....
(*signature of person authorised to sign contracts on behalf of the Employer*)

in the presence of
.... (*signature of witness*)
.... (*name of witness*)
.... (*witness' occupation*)
.... (*witness' address*)

(*Execution in accordance with the legislation governing the authority, or articles of association if a company*)

The Contractor

Given under the Contractor's common seal

....

....   affix Contractor's common seal
(*signatures of persons authorised to authenticate the seal*)

OR **Signed, sealed and delivered** by
.... (*name of attorney*)
as lawful attorney of the Contractor   ....
under a power of attorney dated ....   (*signature of attorney*)
                                                      affix attorney's personal seal

in the presence of
.... (*signature of witness*)
.... (*name of witness*)
.... (*witness' occupation*)
.... (*witness' address*)

OR (*if the Contractor is an individual*)
Signed, sealed and delivered by   ....
.... (*name of Contractor*)   (*signature of Contractor*)

in the presence of
.... (*signature of witness*)
.... (*name of witness*)   affix Contractor's personal seal
.... (*witness' occupation*)
.... (*witness' address*)

NOTE *If the Contractor is a company that is not a company incorporated in Ireland, execution will be in accordance with the law of its jurisdiction of incorporation for execution of a deed.*

Note: If the Contractor is a partnership or joint venture, execution must be by each member, using the blocks below.

Joint Venture Member 1

Given under the common seal of

.... (*name of joint venture member* 1)

....

....

(*signatures of persons authorised to authenticate the seal*)

affix common seal

OR Signed, sealed and delivered by

.... (*name of attorney*)

as lawful attorney of ....

(*name of joint venture member* 1)

under a power of attorney dated ....

....

(*signature of attorney*)

affix attorney's personal seal

in the presence of

.... (*signature of witness*)

.... (*name of witness*)

.... (*witness' occupation*)

.... (*witness' address*)

Joint Venture Member 2

Given under the common seal of

.... (*name of joint venture member* 2)

....

....

(*signatures of persons authorised to authenticate the seal*)

affix common seal

OR Signed, sealed and delivered by

.... (*name of attorney*)

as lawful attorney of ....

(*name of joint venture member* 2)

under a power of attorney dated ....

....

(*signature of attorney*)

affix attorney's personal seal

in the presence of

.... (*signature of witness*)

.... (*name of witness*)

.... (*witness' occupation*)

.... (*witness' address*)

Joint Venture Member 3

Given under the common seal of

.... (*name of joint venture member 3*)

affix common seal

....
....
(*signatures of persons authorised to authenticate the seal*)

OR **Signed, sealed and delivered** by

.... (*name of attorney*)
as lawful attorney of ....
(*name of joint venture member 3*)

under a power of attorney dated ....

....
(*signature of attorney*)
affix attorney's personal seal

in the presence of

.... (*signature of witness*)
.... (*name of witness*)
.... (*witness' occupation*)
.... (*witness' address*)

NOTE If a member of the joint venture is a company that is not a company incorporated in Ireland, execution will be in accordance with the law of its jurisdiction of incorporation for execution of a deed.

GENERAL NOTE

The first part of the Contract sets out the Articles of Agreement. This is the basic Contract and describes what the Contractor agrees to do and the price the Employer agrees to pay to the Contractor. The Articles of Agreement set out the fundamental relationship between the Contractor and the Employer.

There are six Articles expressing the Contract. Between them they establish that this is a Fixed Price Lump Sum Contract, and that in exchange for the Contract Sum the Contractor will carry out the Works in accordance with the Contract Documents. Article 4 sets out that, in calculating the Tender Price, the Contractor has taken into account "all risks, customs, policies, practises and other circumstances that may effect the performance of the Contract, whether foreseen or unforeseen", unless the Contract specifies otherwise. The Contract allows the Employer to decide whether the Contractor will be responsible for unforeseen ground conditions, archaeology and utilities. These risks are detailed in Section K of the Schedule, Part 1, at Items 18 to 21. Therefore, risks to be assumed by the Employer are specified in the Contract – the Contractor deals with everything else.

The Contract Sum is inserted as VAT inclusive and is referred to as a lump sum to be adjusted only when the Contract says so. Only events for which the Contract provides adjustment of the initial Contract Sum will be allowed.

CONDITIONS

1. THE CONTRACT

1.1 Definitions

The following terms have the following meanings in the Contract:

Change Order means an instruction of the Employer's Representative to change [including add to or omit from] the Works or to change [including impose or remove] constraints in the Contract on how the Works are to be executed.

Consent means planning permission, order, approval, certificate, fire certificate, licence, permit, environmental impact statement, or other consent required by Law for the execution or completion of the Works, or identified as a Consent in the Works Requirements.

Contract Date means the date the Employer issued the Letter of Acceptance.

Contract Sum means the amount identified in the Agreement as the initial Contract Sum, as adjusted in accordance with the Contract.

Contractor's Documents means drawings, specifications, manuals, reports and other [eye readable and machine readable] written material relating to the Works that the Contractor uses, prepares or gives to the Employer or any other person, or is to use, prepare or give to the Employer or any other person

- under the Works Requirements or

- under any Legal Requirement or

- to obtain any Consent or

- in connection with a proposal under sub-clause 4.8.

> **NOTE**
>
> "Contractor's Documents" means drawings, specifications, manuals, reports and other written material relating to the Works. This could be the Contractor's applications for Consents under the Contract for which he may be responsible. Such responsibilities will be contained within the Contract Documents.

Contractor's Things means equipment, facilities and other things the Contractor [or Contractor's Personnel] uses on or adjacent to the Site to execute the Works, except Works Items.

Contractor's Personnel means the Contractor's representative, supervisor and Subcontractors, employees and other persons working on or adjacent to the Site for the Contractor or Subcontractors, and other persons assisting the Contractor to perform the Contract.

Date for Substantial Completion of the Works or a Section means the date identified as the Date for Substantial Completion of the Works or Section in the Schedule, part 1G or 2D, and, if the Schedule states a period, the last day of that period, starting on the Contract Date, in either case as adjusted in accordance with the Contract.

Defect means non-compliance of the Works or a Works Item with the Contract [including a failed test and, after Substantial Completion, work that has not been completed].

Defects Certificate means a certificate of the Employer's Representative that the Defects Period has ended.

Defects Period means the period starting on Substantial Completion of the Works and continuing for the period stated in the Schedule, as may be extended under sub-clause 8.6.2.

Designated Date means the date 10 days before the last day for receipt of the Contractor's tender for the Works, or, if there was none, 10 days before the Employer received the Contractor's tender for the Works.

Employer's Personnel means any of the following:

- the Employer's Representative

- the Employer's employees, agents and consultants in connection with the Contract when acting on behalf of the Employer but not when exercising authority under Law

- other contractors of the Employer working on the Site when acting within the scope of their contracts with the Employer

- anyone else the Employer's Representative notifies the Contractor is Employer's Personnel.

> **NOTE**
>
> Employer's Personnel can also include other contractors engaged by the Employer on the site.

Employer's Representative means the architect, engineer, quantity surveyor or other person appointed by the Employer as its representative in accordance with the Contract.

Law means enactments and statutory instruments, each as defined by the Interpretation Act 2005, and regulations, directives and decisions of the European Union having direct effect in Ireland.

Legal Requirement means a requirement that applies to the Works as a result of any of the following:

- Law

- a Consent

- a decision of an Irish court, the European Court of Justice or the European Court of First Instance

- the requirements of any person having authority in connection with the Works under any Law

- the requirements of any person with whose systems the Works will connect

- the legal rights of any person.

Letter of Acceptance means the Employer's letter to the Contractor accepting the Tender.

Section means a part of the Works identified as a Section in the Schedule, part 1G.

Site means any place

- where the Works are to be executed according to the Contract or

- provided by the Employer for the Works or

- where the Contractor is to operate or maintain Employer's facilities or

- that the Works Requirements identify as part of the Site.

Site Working Day means a day on which, according to the Contract and the Contractor's programme most recently submitted to the Employer's Representative, the Contractor is to execute the Works on the Site.

> **NOTE**
>
> Site Working Day, as opposed to "working day", is a day indicted to be a working day by the last accepted programme. It is an important definition as it is only site working days for which an extension of time can be allowed. It has a particular effect on claims occurring during a holiday period: if they are not taken for in the programme they may be ignored in the calculation of the extension of time.

Specialist means any of the following:

- a Subcontractor or supplier of a Works Item named in the Contract
- Contractor's Personnel who do or are to do design
- Contractor's Personnel stated in the Works Requirements to be Specialists.

Starting Date means the day the Contractor proposes to start executing the Works, as notified by the Contractor to the Employer's Representative under sub-clause 9.1.

Subcontractor means a person to whom the execution of part of the Works is subcontracted [by the Contractor or another Subcontractor].

Substantial Completion of the Works or a part of the Works [including a Section] means that all of the following have happened:

(1)   the Works or the part of the Works are complete so that they can be taken over and used by the Employer for their intended purpose and there are no Defects other than

    (a)   Defects accepted by the Employer under sub-clause 8.5.4 or

    (b)   minor Defects to which all of the following apply:

        (i)   they do not prevent the Works or the part from being used for their intended purpose

        (ii)   the Employer's Representative considers the Contractor has reasonable grounds for not promptly rectifying them

        (iii)   rectification will not prejudice the safe and convenient use of the Works or the part

(2)   all tests that are required by the Contract to be passed before Substantial Completion have been passed

(3)   the Contractor has given the Employer's Representative the Contractor's Documents that the Contract requires be provided before Substantial Completion

(4)   the Contractor has given the Employer's Representative the collateral warranties that the Contract requires for the Works or part.

NOTE

Substantial Completion includes conditions that all tests required have been completed and passed before Substantial Completion can occur. The Contractor must provide the documents as required by the Contract to the Employer or Employer's Representative including all collateral warranties before Substantial Completion can occur. Management and production of all such documentation is essential for the Contractor.

Works Item means a part of the Works, anything that the Contractor intends will become part of the Works, or temporary works for the Works.

1.2   Interpretation

1.2.1   The parties intend the Contract to be given purposeful meaning for efficiency and public benefit generally and as particularly identified in the Contract.

1.2.2   Unless the context indicates otherwise, in the Contract

    1.   References to the Works are to the works described in the Works Requirements.

    2.   Words in the singular include the plural and vice versa.

    3.   References to an **individual** are to a human person.

4.   References to a **person** include human persons and corporate and unincorporated bodies.

5.   Words in any gender include all genders.

6.   References to any **Law** include amendments and replacements.

7.   References to the **Contract** or any other writing include amendments.

8.   References to a **day** mean a calendar day.

9.   References to a **week** mean a period of 7 days.

10.   References to a **month** mean a calendar month.

11.   References to a **working day** mean a day that is not Saturday, Sunday, a public holiday established under the Organisation of Working Time Act 1997 or Good Friday.

12.   References to a requirement to **submit** a document or proposed course of action to Employer's Representative mean to submit it according to sub-clause 4.7, or another procedure that applies according to the Works Requirements, and sub-clause 4.7 or the Works Requirements shall apply in every such case. [Accordingly the Contractor may not implement the submission until permitted by sub-clause 4.7 or the Works Requirements].

13.   References to the Contractor's **current programme** are to the programme in the Works Proposals, if there is one, if not, to the programme first submitted by the Contractor under sub-clause 4.9, or, in either case, to any later programme submitted by the Contractor if the period for the Employer's Representative to review it has passed and there is no outstanding objection.

14.   References to **liability** include claims, demands and proceedings.

15.   Terms such as **including, in particular, such as**, and **for example**, are not to be read as exhaustive, or to limit, but may extend, the generality of the provisions to which they relate.

16.   References to the **Agreement** and **Schedule** are to the attached agreement and completed schedule.

17.   References to the **Works Requirements, Works Proposals** and the **Pricing Document** are to the Works Requirements, Works Proposals and Pricing Document identified in the Schedule, parts 1B and 2C; in the case of Works Requirements, as changed by Change Orders; and in the case of Works Proposals, as changed under sub-clause 4.6.2.

18.   References to **Delay Events** and **Compensation Events** are to events identified as Delay Events and Compensation Events in the Schedule, part 1K.

19.   References to the **initial** Contract Sum are to the Contract Sum stated in the Agreement; references to an initial Date for Substantial Completion are to a Date for Substantial Completion identified in the Schedule; and references to the initial Works Requirements are to the Works Requirements identified in the Schedule.

1.2.3   Clarifications, examples and reminders are included occasionally in square brackets to show that no significance is to be given to their absence elsewhere.

1.3   Inconsistencies

1.3.1   Except when the Contract states otherwise, the documents in the Contract are to be taken as mutually explanatory of each other if possible. If there is an inconsistency between the documents, they take precedence as follows:

First, the Agreement, even if it has not been executed

Second, the Letter of Acceptance and any post-tender clarifications listed in it

Third, the Schedule

Fourth, these Conditions

Fifth, the Works Requirements

Sixth, the Pricing Document

Seventh, the Works Proposals, if there are any

Eighth, any other documents in the Contract

1.3.2 If either party becomes aware of any inconsistency between terms of the Contract, it shall promptly inform the other party.

1.3.3 If there is an inconsistency between figured and scaled dimensions, the figured dimensions prevail.

1.3.4 If the Works Requirements include a Bill of Quantities, and the Bill of Quantities is inconsistent with any other Works Requirements, the other Works Requirements prevail.

> **NOTE**
> Inconsistencies should be promptly notified. No action is identified in the Contract, however precedence of documents applies. The status of the Bills of Quantities will be identified within the Contract Documents.

1.4 Pricing Document and Works Proposals

Nothing in and no omission from the Pricing Document or Works Proposals limits the scope of the Works or the Contractor's obligations. Nothing in the Pricing Document or Works Proposals imposes obligations on the Employer.

1.5 Performance Bond

Before the Starting Date, unless the Schedule, part 1E, says that no bond is required, the Contractor shall give the Employer a performance bond in the form in the Works Requirements, or, if there is none, a form approved by the Employer. The performance bond shall be in the amount stated in the Schedule, part 1E, and shall be executed by the Contractor and by a surety approved by the Employer.

> **NOTE**
> Any performance bond is to be delivered before the start date notified by the Contractor. That will normally be within four weeks of the issue of the Letter of Acceptance.
> The same requirement applies to any parent company guarantee required.
> Bonds and guarantees are to comply with model forms contained within the Contract Documents.

1.6 Parent Company Guarantee

If the Schedule, part 2B, says that there is to be a parent company guarantee, the Contractor shall give the Employer such a guarantee before the Starting Date. It shall be executed by the parent company named in the Schedule, part 2B, and in the form in the Works Requirements, or, if there is none, a form approved by the Employer.

1.7 Joint Ventures

If the Contractor is a joint venture, consortium or other unincorporated grouping of two or more persons, those persons shall be jointly and severally liable to the Employer for the performance of the Contract.

1.8   Assignment

The Contractor may not assign the benefit of the Contract, or any part of it, without the Employer's consent.

1.9   Miscellaneous

1.9.1   The Contract and the documents referred to in it supersede all previous representations, arrangements, understandings and agreements between the parties about the subject-matter of the Contract, and set out the entire agreement between the parties about the subject-matter of the Contract. Neither party has relied on any other written or oral representation, arrangement, understanding or agreement.

1.9.2   All the terms of the Contract are severable, and if any part is unenforceable, illegal or void, it is to that extent considered not to form part of the Contract, and the enforceability, legality and validity of the rest of the Contract will not be affected.

1.9.3   The Contract may only be changed by a document in writing signed by an authorised representative of each party.

> **NOTE**
>
> This confirms that any changes to the Contract Documents can only be effected when made in writing by authorised persons.

1.9.4   The rights of a party will not be prejudiced or restricted by any indulgence or forbearance extended to the other party, and no waiver by a party of any breach will waive any other breach. No failure or delay by a party in exercising any right or remedy will waive the right or remedy, nor will any single or partial exercise or waiver of any right or remedy prejudice any other exercise of that or any other right or remedy.

> **GENERAL NOTE ON SECTION**
>
> This section of the Contract deals with how the parties are to read and interpret the Contract and how the Contract Documents will be treated.

2 THE LAW

2.1 Law Governing the Contract

Irish law governs the Contract and its interpretation.

2.2 Compliance with Legal Requirements

The Contractor shall in performing the Contract comply with all Legal Requirements and ensure that the Contractor's Personnel comply with all Legal Requirements.

2.3 Consents

2.3.1 The Employer has obtained, or shall obtain, the Consents that the Works Requirements say that the Employer is to obtain. The Contractor shall obtain all other Consents.

2.3.2 The Contractor shall give and comply with all notices and pay all taxes, fees and charges required under Legal Requirements to be paid in connection with performing the Contract, unless the Works Requirements say otherwise.

2.4 Project Supervisor

2.4.1 If the Works Requirements say that the Contractor is to be appointed project supervisor for the construction stage in accordance with the Safety, Health and Welfare at Work (Construction) Regulations 2006 (the **Construction Regulations**) for the Works, or a project including the Works, the Contractor shall accept the appointment by entering into the appointment in the form in the Works Requirements. If the Works Requirements say that an individual or body corporate named in the Works Proposals is to be appointed project supervisor for the construction stage in accordance with the Construction Regulations for the Works, or a project including the Works, the Contractor shall ensure that the individual or body corporate named in the Works Proposals accepts the appointment by entering into the appointment in the form in the Works Requirements. The Contractor shall, if appointed as project supervisor, comply with its obligations under the Construction Regulations in connection with that appointment. If the Employer terminates the appointment of the Contractor or other person named in the Works Proposals as project supervisor for the construction stage as a result of that project supervisor's failure to comply with its obligations, the Contractor shall pay to the Employer all the Employer's cost resulting from the termination [including the cost of appointing and fees and expenses paid to a replacement project supervisor, or, if the Employer acts as project supervisor itself, the Employer's cost of doing so].

> **NOTE**
>
> If a Contractor takes on the role of Project Supervisor and fails to adequately perform, resource and provide the necessary insurances the Employer may terminate the Contractor's role and appoint another party to carry out the duties of project supervisor (construction stage). In the event of the contractor being replaced in this role the Contractor is responsible for all the Employer's costs involved in the new appointment.

2.4.2 If the Contractor or a person named in the Works Proposals is to be appointed as project supervisor for the construction stage, the Contractor represents and warrants to the Employer that the Contractor or person named in the Works Proposals is competent and will allocate adequate resources to enable itself to perform its duties under the Construction Regulations.

2.4.3 If the Contractor or a person named in the Works Proposals is appointed as project supervisor for the construction stage the Contractor shall ensure that the project supervisor has the insurances required of the project supervisor under its appointment.

NOTE

If the Employer appoints a person other than the Contractor as Project Supervisor, the Contractor is obliged to comply with all the requirements of the Project Supervisor.

2.4.4 The Contractor shall [without adjustment to the Contract Sum or extension of time] comply with all the lawful directions of the project supervisors appointed for the construction stage and the design process in accordance with the Construction Regulations for the Works, or any project including the Works, and give them any copies of Contractor's Documents that they may request.

2.5   Safety, Health and Welfare at Work Act 2005 and Safety, Health and Welfare at Work (Construction) Regulations 2006

2.5.1 The Contractor shall [without limiting other obligations] ensure, so far as is reasonably practicable, that the Works are constructed to be safe and without risk to health, and that the Works comply in all respects, as appropriate, with the relevant statutory provisions.

2.5.2 The Contractor represents and warrants to the Employer that the Contractor is, and will, while performing the Contract, be a competent person for the purpose of ensuring, so far as is reasonably practicable, that the Works are constructed to be safe and without risk to health and that they comply in all respects, as appropriate, with the relevant statutory provisions.

2.5.3 The Contractor represents and warrants to the Employer that the Contractor is and will, while performing the Contract, be a competent person to carry out the Works and has allocated and will allocate sufficient resources to enable itself to comply with the requirements and prohibitions imposed on the Contractor by or under the relevant statutory provisions.

2.5.4 In this sub-clause 2.5 and sub-clause 2.4, **competent person, reasonably practicable** and **relevant statutory provisions** are construed according to section 2 of the Safety, Health and Welfare at Work Act 2005.

2.6   Ethics in Public Office

The Contractor warrants that

2.6.1 neither the Contractor nor any person on the Contractor's behalf has offered, given or agreed to give to the Employer or to any of the Employer's Personnel any gift or consideration of any kind in connection with the Contract, nor will they make such an offer, gift or agreement and

2.6.2 neither the Contractor nor any person on the Contractor's behalf has committed any offence under the Prevention of Corruption Acts 1889 to 2001 or the Ethics in Public Office Acts 1995 and 2001 in connection with the Contract, nor will they commit any such offence and

2.6.3 no Minister of the Government or Minister of State, or officer or employee of the Employer, will have or receive any share or part of the Contract or any benefit from the Contract and

2.6.4 unless fully disclosed to and agreed by the Employer in advance

   (1)   no former officer nor employee of the Employer nor of a consultant to the Employer whose duties related to the Works will, for 12 months after leaving the employment or office, be engaged as Contractor's Personnel and

(2)   no consultant or former consultant to the Employer whose duties related to the Works will be engaged as Contractor's Personnel, except for a Specialist whose contract is to be novated from the Employer to the Contractor.

> **NOTE**
>
> This sub-clause deals with ethics in public office which contain restrictions as to the employment of personnel, including consultants, who were formerly engaged on the Works by the Employer. The sub-clause contains a prohibition on their working for the Contractor.

2.7   Legal Opinion

2.7.1   If the Contractor or any person executing a bond, guarantee, warranty or other deed or agreement required by the Contract is not an individual or a company incorporated in Ireland the Contractor shall give the Employer, together with the Agreement or other document, a legal opinion that

(1)   the Contractor, or other counterparty, is an entity duly incorporated under the laws of its place of incorporation and is a separate legal entity, capable of being sued in its own name, is validly existing under the laws of that place and no steps have been taken or are being taken to appoint a receiver, examiner, administrator, liquidator, trustee or similar person over it or to wind it up and

(2)   the Contractor has the necessary power and authority, and all necessary corporate and other action has been taken, to give it the power to execute, deliver and perform the obligations undertaken by it under the Contract or other document and

(3)   the Contract, or other document, has been duly executed by the Contractor, or other counterparty, or on its behalf, and is binding on it under the laws of the place where it is incorporated and

(4)   a judgment of an Irish court will be enforceable against the Contractor, or other counterparty, in the place where it is incorporated.

2.7.2   The opinion shall be written by a lawyer, approved by the Employer, who is authorised to practice in the place where the counterparty is incorporated. The opinion shall be in a form approved by the Employer. It shall be addressed to the Employer.

> **GENERAL NOTE ON THIS SECTION**
>
> This section sets out the Contractor's legal obligation to carry out the Contract in accordance with the law, legal requirements and Consents obtained and to be obtained in connection with the Works Requirements.
>
> This section, for the first time in Irish standard forms of construction contracts, introduce the requirements in relation to health, safety and welfare legislation. It is under this section that the risk of changes in legislation is passed to the Contractor.
>
> It is in this section that the risks of Consents are transferred to the Contractor. The Contractor shall be informed of the Consents for which the Employer will be responsible. All other Consents will be the responsibility of the Contractor including costs both of obtaining the Consents themselves and any delay incurred while awaiting the Consents.

3 LOSS, DAMAGE AND INJURY

3.1 Employer's Risks of Loss and Damage to the Works

The Employer shall bear the risk of loss of or damage to the Works resulting from any of the following:

(1) war, invasion, act of foreign enemies, hostilities whether war is declared or not, civil war, rebellion, revolution, insurrection, military or usurped power

(2) pressure waves caused by aircraft or other airborne objects travelling at sonic or supersonic speeds

(3) contamination by radioactivity or radioactive, toxic, explosive or other hazardous properties of any explosive nuclear assembly or its components, in each case not caused by the Contractor or the Contractor's Personnel

(4) terrorism, but only if terrorism is a permitted exclusion from the Contractor's insurance of the Works

(5) use or occupation of the Works by the Employer or the Employer's Personnel, other than

(i) as provided for in the Contract or

(ii) to the extent that the loss or damage is caused by the negligence of the Contractor or the Contractor's Personnel, or the Contractor's breach of the Contract (subject to sub-clause 3.8 if it applies)

(6) design of the Works by the Employer or Employer's Personnel, but not if the design is covered by insurance required under the Contract.

3.2 Care of the Works

3.2.1 The Contractor shall have full responsibility for the care of, and risk of loss of and damage to, the Works, Works Items, Contractor's Things, Works Requirements, Works Proposals, Contractor's Documents, and anything the Employer gives the Contractor for the Works (together, **Risk Items**) from and including the Starting Date until and including the date the Employer's Representative issues the certificate of Substantial Completion of the Works (or in respect of a Section, the date the Employer's Representative issues the certificate of Substantial Completion of the Section, or in respect of a part of the Works that the Employer takes over under sub-clause 9.7, the date the Employer takes over the part). After that date, the Contractor shall be responsible for loss of and damage to Risk Items due to any of the following:

(1) Defects

(2) occurrences before the Employer's Representative issued the certificate of Substantial Completion (or, where applicable, before the Employer took over the part)

(3) activities of the Contractor or Contractor's Personnel.

(4) But the Contractor's responsibility under this sub-clause 3.2 excludes loss of and damage to the Works that is at the Employer's risk under sub-clause 3.1.

3.2.2 The Contractor shall promptly rectify any loss and damage to Risk Items for which it is responsible under this sub-clause 3.2 [at its own expense if there are not sufficient insurance proceeds].

3.2.3 If loss of or damage to the Works, for which the Contractor is not responsible under this sub-clause 3.2, occurs before the Defects Certificate is issued, the Contractor shall rectify it in accordance with any instruction of the Employer.

3.3   Insurance of the Works

3.3.1   From the Starting Date, the Contractor shall insure the Works and other Risk Items against loss and damage. The insurance shall name the Contractor, the Employer and any other persons the Employer requires as co-insured. The insurance shall be kept in place for each Section until the date that the certificate of Substantial Completion of the Section is issued, and for the Works, except Sections that have a certificate of Substantial Completion, until the date that the certificate of Substantial Completion of the Works is issued. If so required in the Schedule, part 1D, the insurance for any Section or part of the Works that has reached Substantial Completion shall be extended until the Employer's Representative certifies Substantial Completion of the whole of the Works. In any event, after Substantial Completion, the insurance shall be kept in place until the Defects Certificate is issued, to cover loss and damage for which the Contractor remains responsible under the Contract. The limit of the insurance shall be, except for loss of or damage to Contractor's Things and Employer's property, for the full reinstatement cost of the property insured, including the cost of demolition, removal of debris, delivery, professional fees, inflation occurring during the construction and reinstatement periods, and profit. The sum insured for professional fees shall include at least the percentage of the Contract Sum stated in the Schedule, part 1D. The insurance shall include any Employer's property listed in the Schedule, part 1D, and the indemnity limit for those items shall be as stated in the Schedule.

3.3.2   The proceeds of the insurance of the Works, less the portion to cover professional fees that the Employer is to pay, shall be paid into a bank account in the joint names of the Employer and the Contractor. They shall be paid out of the account to the Contractor in instalments on the basis of interim payment certificates of the Employer's Representative of the Contract value of the work done and Works Items delivered to the Site to rectify the loss or damage, following generally sub-clause 11.1, and also paid out of the account to the Employer for its other costs. Any balance remaining in the account after the work of rectification is complete shall be paid to the Employer.

3.4   Contractor's Indemnity

3.4.1   The Contractor shall indemnify the Employer and the Employer's employees against

(1)   liability and

(2)   loss of and damage to the Employer's property [including the Site], unless excluded under sub-clause 3.8

arising from or in the course of the Contractor's performance or non-performance of the Contract.

3.4.2   The Contractor's indemnity in this sub-clause 3.4 does not apply to the Employer's liability under the Contract to the Contractor; nor does it apply to liability to the extent that the liability is covered by the Employer's indemnities in sub-clauses 3.5 and 6.2.

3.4.3   The Contractor's indemnity for liability for death, injury or illness of any Contractor's Personnel shall apply regardless of whether the death, illness or injury was caused wholly or in part by the negligence of the Employer or any Employer's Personnel.

3.5   Employer's Indemnity

The Employer shall indemnify the Contractor against liability the Contractor incurs in the course of performing the Contract, to the extent that the liability is

(1)   caused by the negligence of the Employer or

(2)   for property damage that is the unavoidable result of executing the Works in accordance with the Works Requirements.

But this indemnity does not cover liability for death, injury or illness of Contractor's Personnel.

3.6   Public Liability and Employer's Liability insurances

3.6.1 From the Starting Date until the date the Defects Certificate is issued, the Contractor shall insure the Employer and the Contractor as co-insured against their respective liabilities for

(1) death, injury or illness of any person and

(2) loss of or damage to any physical property and

(3) obstruction, loss of amenities, nuisance, trespass, stoppage of traffic and infringement of light, easement or quasi-easement

resulting from an accident arising from or in the course of the performance or non-performance of the Contract.

3.6.2 From the Starting Date until the date the Defects Certificate is issued, the Contractor shall insure itself against liability for death, injury or illness of Contractor's Personnel. For employees of Subcontractors, this obligation may be satisfied by ensuring that the Subcontractor maintains the insurance. The Contractor shall ensure that this insurance includes a provision that indemnifies the Employer against any liability for which the Contractor would be entitled to an indemnity, including costs, charges and expenses.

3.6.3 The minimum indemnity limit of the Contractor's public liability and employer's liability insurances shall be as stated in the Schedule, part 1D.

3.6.4 If the Contractor or the Contractor's Personnel return to the Site in connection with the Works after the Defects Certificate is issued, the Contractor shall ensure the insurances required by this sub-clause 3.6 are in place at all times that the Contractor or Contractor's Personnel are on Site.

3.7   Professiona l Indemnity Insurance

If the Schedule states that professional indemnity insurance is required, from the Starting Date until the sixth anniversary of the date that the Employer's Representative certifies Substantial Completion of the Works, or any other period stated in the Schedule, part 1D, the Contractor shall maintain professional indemnity insurance for its performance of the Contract. The indemnity limit shall be at least that stated in the Schedule, part 1D. This insurance shall include retroactive cover to when the Contractor's design of the Works and Works Items started.

3.8   Existing Facilities and Use or Occupation by Employer

This sub-clause 3.8 shall apply only if so stated in the Schedule, part 1D.

To the extent that the Works involve alteration or extension of existing facilities owned by the Employer, and to the extent that the Employer uses or occupies the Works, the Employer shall bear the risk of loss of or damage to those facilities and the part of the Works used or occupied by the Employer, and their contents owned by the Employer, caused by any of the following perils, as defined in the Works Requirements or, if not defined there, in standard fire and specified perils insurance policies available in Ireland:

(1) fire, storm, tempest, flood

(2) bursting or overflowing of water tanks, apparatus or pipes

(3) explosion, impact, aircraft

(4) riot, civil commotion or malicious damage.

3.9   General Requirements Concerning Insurance

3.9.1   The insurance required by the Contract (the **Insurance**) shall be placed with reputable insurers approved by the Employer.

3.9.2   The only exclusions from the Insurance shall be those listed in the Schedule, part 1D. The levels of excess shall be no higher than stated in the Schedule, part 1D.

3.9.3   The Insurance shall include any extensions and comply with any additional requirements in the Schedule and the Works Requirements.

3.9.4   Liability Insurance on which the Employer is required to be co-insured shall include a cross-liability clause. All Insurance on which the Employer is required to be co-insured shall provide that

(1)   the insurer accepts the term "insured" as applying to each insured person as if a separate policy of insurance had been issued to each of them, but without the overall limit of indemnity being increased as a result, and that non-compliance by the Contractor or any other co-insured will not affect the Employer's rights and

(2)   the insurer agrees to waive all rights of subrogation or action against any of the persons who are insured.

3.9.5   The Contractor shall comply with the terms of the Insurance policies.

3.9.6   Within 10 working days of being requested to do so, the Contractor shall give the Employer evidence to the Employer's satisfaction that the Insurances are in effect, including copies of policies and receipts for premiums. For professional indemnity insurance, a certificate in the form included in the Works Requirements, or, if there is none, a form approved by the Employer, signed by the broker or underwriter, may be given instead of a copy of the professional indemnity policy.

3.9.7   The Contractor shall not make any material reduction to the Insurance cover unless approved in advance by the Employer. The Contractor shall promptly notify the Employer of any cancellation, renewal, non-renewal or material reduction by the insurer of any Insurance policy.

3.9.8   If the Contractor fails to maintain any of the Insurances in the terms required by the Contract, the Employer shall be entitled [without affecting its other rights] to take out the insurance and pay the premiums, and the Contractor shall pay the amount of the premiums to the Employer on demand.

3.9.9   If the Works Requirements include provision for an owner controlled insurance programme, the parties shall comply with those provisions, including any amendments they make to this clause 3.

GENERAL NOTE ON SECTION

This section of the Contract sets out the risks each party will bear in respect of loss or damage to the Works and includes the insurance requirements and the Contractor's obligation to take care of the Works both during the life of the project and after Practical Completion until the Defects Certificate is issued by the Employer's Representative.

The indemnities to be provided by the Contractor and the Employer are detailed, including the fact that the Employer may require Professional Indemnity cover for any element of design to be carried out by the Contractor his personnel.

The definition of "liability" under this Contract is broad. It is possible that the indemnity provisions may extend to a Contractor's liability to consequential and indirect losses incurred. Contractors should seek advice from their brokers or insurance agents on these provisions.

The Contractor must have the required insurances in place before the start date. Evidence of such has to be produced within 10 working days of a request from the Employer, copies of policies and receipts for premiums paid. From a contract-administration point of view, no change in insurance levels is allowed without advance notice and approval from the Employer. The Employer, on default, can take out his own insurance and recover the cost from the Contractor. The Employer may require the Contractor to extend his All Risks insurance to cover the Employer's own facilities and contents for standard perils. Contractor's should note that terrorism and asbestos indemnities may be listed as possible exclusions.

4 MANAGEMENT

4.1 Co-Operation

4.1.1 The Employer [subject to restraints as a public authority] and the Contractor shall support reciprocal co-operation for the Contract purposes, including co-operation with and between Contractor's Personnel and Employer's Personnel.

4.1.2 Such support may be relevant particularly to any of the following:

(1) negotiation of agreements provided for in the Contract

(2) value engineering

(3) use of most effective and compatible electronic and other methods of communicating and recording

(4) efficient order and timing of information provided for in the Contract

(5) minimising the effects of suspension

(6) efforts by the Contractor to minimise delay and Compensation Events and their effects

(7) Contractor's flexible management

4.1.3 Either party, or the Employer's Representative, may request clarifications, consultations, workshops, exchange of information and expertise, or investigations, although not provided for elsewhere in the Contract. The request shall specify purposes and, as relevant, proposed participants, arrangements, methods and any proposals for recording or agreeing results.

> **NOTE**
>
> This sub-clause provides a useful facility to have all matters or any contentious matters examined to determine the basis of any instruction or decision of the Employer's Representative.

4.1.4 The parties may agree to consult or communicate, without prejudice. In any case, offering or giving co-operation does not imply any admission of any responsibility or alter either party's rights or duties unless otherwise agreed in writing.

4.2 Contractor's Representative and Supervisor

4.2.1 The Contractor shall appoint, before the Starting Date

(1) a representative with full authority to act on behalf of the Contractor in all matters concerning the Contract and

(2) a full-time supervisor of all the Contractor's activities on the Site, with full authority to receive instructions and other communications on behalf of the Contractor in all matters concerning the Contract.

The representative and the supervisor may, but need not, be the same person.

4.2.2 Matters of which the Contractor's representative or supervisor are aware [including communications and instructions] are presumed to be within the Contractor's knowledge.

4.2.3 If the Contractor's representative or supervisor are named in the Works Proposals, the Contractor shall appoint the individuals named. If not, or either of them is changed, the Contractor shall submit details of the proposed representative or supervisor to the Employer's Representative. If the Contractor's representative or supervisor dies, or becomes incapable of performing their role, or is no longer available to the Contractor, the Contractor shall appoint a suitable replacement, having submitted details to the Employer's Representative. If the Employer's Representative so requires because of the misconduct, negligence or incompetence of either of them, the Contractor shall remove its representative or supervisor and appoint a suitable replacement, having submitted details to the Employer's Representative.

> **NOTE**
>
> This sub-clause deals with the Contractor's supervision. The Contractor must notify the Employer's Representative of the name of the Contractor's representative or supervisor before the start date. If named in the Work Proposals, they shall be the persons appointed unless a change is notified to the Employer's Representative. The Employer's Representative has the power to have the Contractor remove a Contractor's representative or supervisor arising from misconduct, negligence or incompetence. The Contractor shall comply with the Employer's Representative's requirement having submitted details to the Employer's Representative.

4.3   Employer's Representative

4.3.1   If the Employer's Representative is not named in the Schedule, part 1A, the Employer shall, promptly after the Contract Date, appoint, and notify the Contractor of the identity of, the Employer's Representative.

4.3.2   If there are limitations on the authority of the Employer's Representative to perform its functions or powers under the Contract, they are stated in the Contract. But any act or instruction of the Employer's Representative under the Contract shall have effect as if within the Employer's Representative's authority, and the Contractor need not inquire into whether the Employer has actually authorised it.

4.3.3   The Employer's Representative may delegate in writing to named representatives any functions or powers under the Contract and revoke any delegation. The appointment of such a representative shall not prevent the Employer's Representative from exercising directly any functions or powers. The Employer's Representative shall notify the Contractor and the Employer of any delegation, and the names of representatives, and of any subsequent changes, within 5 working days after the event in each case.

4.3.4   Any opinion, certificate, determination, assessment or objection of the Employer's Representative under the Contract may be revised in accordance with clause 13, except for decisions stated in the Contract to be conclusive [such as rejection of a value engineering proposal under sub-clause 4.8 or rejection of a Defect under sub-clause 8.5.4].

4.3.5   The Employer may replace the Employer's Representative at any time, notifying the Contractor of the replacement, and shall do so promptly if the position of Employer's Representative becomes vacant before the Defects Certificate (or alternatively the certificates required following termination) have been issued. Pending appointment of a replacement, the Employer shall carry out the functions and powers of the Employer's Representative.

4.4   Employer's Representative's communications

4.4.1   The Employer's Representative may give the Contractor

     (1)   instructions, which are either

         (a)   directions in accordance with the Contract or

         (b)   Change Orders and

     (2)   objections, in accordance with sub-clause 4.7.

4.4.2   The Employer's Representative may give the Contractor or the Employer, or both

(1)   opinions, assessments, determinations and certificates, in accordance with the Contract and

(2)   other communications [including clarifications] in accordance with the Contract or the Employer's Representative considers appropriate.

> **NOTE**
>
> The Employer's Representative may give the Contractor instructions which can be either:
>
> (i)   Directions in accordance with the Contract; or
>
> (ii)   Change Orders.
>
> The Employer's Representative may also object to any of the Contractor's proposals in accordance with sub-clause 4.7.
>
> The Employer's Representative may also give opinions, assessments, determinations and certificates in accordance with the Contract and other communications, including clarifications, in accordance with the Contract or as the Employer's Representative considers appropriate.
>
> Despite the apparent restrictions mentioned under the Schedule in Part 1A, the Employer's Representative has similar powers to both the engineer and architect under the IEI or GDLA forms. The Employer's Representative may issue instructions up to the issue of the Defects certificate. The Employer's Representative may change the Work Requirements, impose, change or remove restrictions on the way the work is done and/or give instructions on defects.
>
> Instructions are to be given to the Contractor when requested in the time required under sub-clause 4.

4.5   Instructions

4.5.1   The Employer's Representative may issue instructions to the Contractor on any matter connected with the Works [whether or not mentioned elsewhere in the Contract] at any time up to the date the Defects Certificate is issued. The Contractor shall comply with an instruction of the Employer's Representative.

4.5.2   If the Employer's Representative gives an instruction and calls it a direction, but the Contractor considers that it is a Change Order, the Contractor shall be entitled to give notice under sub-clause 10.3, and have the issue determined under clause 10. In addition to the requirements of sub-clause 10.3, the Contractor must give this notice before starting to implement the instruction, otherwise it will be taken to be a direction.

4.5.3   The Employer's Representative shall not give a Change Order concerning the Works or a Section after its Substantial Completion has been certified, except concerning Defects or work to be done after Substantial Completion.

4.5.4   The Employer's Representative shall give an instruction that is, in the Employer's Representative's opinion, necessary for the completion of the Works. If, in the Employer's Representative's opinion, it is physically impossible or contrary to Legal Requirements to complete the Works in accordance with the Works Requirements, the Employer's Representative shall give a Change Order. The Employer's Representative shall give an instruction required under this sub-clause 4.5.4 within the time required by sub-clause 4.11.

4.5.5   Instructions of the Employer's Representative shall be given in writing except when there is imminent danger to safety or health or of damage to property, in which case the Employer's Representative may give oral instructions, and shall confirm them in writing as soon as practicable.

> **NOTE**
>
> The Employer's Representative issues all instructions on any matter connected with the Works at any time up to the date the Defects Certificate is issued. The Contractor must comply with all

instructions. There is no facility for the Contractor to confirm or to work on verbal instructions unless on matters of health and safety.

Sub-clause 4.5.2 provides that if the Employer's Representative issues a direction which the Contractor considers to be a Change Order then the Contractor can give notice under clause 10.3 and have the matter determined under clause 10. The Contractor must give this notice before starting to implement the instruction, otherwise it will be taken to be a Direction. The Employer's Representative will make a determination under sub-clause 10.5. The Contractor, if dissatisfied with the Employer's Representative's determination, can refer the matter to conciliation.

All directions should be reviewed to establish if it is a Change Order. In the event of a Change Order being issued then it is a Delay and Compensation Event under Item 1 of Section K of the Schedule, Part 1.

4.6   Works Proposals

4.6.1 The Contractor shall ensure that all Works Proposals comply with the Works Requirements.

4.6.2 If any Works Proposals do not comply with the Contract or the Works Requirements or Legal Requirements or are physically impossible to comply with, the Contractor shall propose a change to the Works Proposals as necessary. [There shall be no extension of time or adjustment to the Contract Sum for this.] If the Works Proposals need to be changed because of a change to the Works Requirements, the Contractor shall propose a change. The Contractor shall submit any change to the Works Proposals to the Employer's Representative.

NOTE

If any Works Proposals do not comply with the Contract or the initial Works Requirements or are physically impossible to comply with, the Contractor shall propose a change to the Works Proposals as necessary. There shall be no extension of time or adjustment to the Contract Sum for this.

Condition 4.6.2 states that "*If the Works Proposals need to be changed because of a change to the Works Requirements, the Contractor shall propose a change. The Contractor shall submit any change to the Works Proposals to the Employer's Representative.*" This proposal comes under Item 1 of Section K of the Schedule and is a Delay Event and a Compensation Event.

Condition 4.6.1 requires the Contractor to provide a statement of the proposed action and all supporting information to the Employer's Representative.

4.7   Required Contractor Submissions

Unless the Works Requirements say that a different procedure is to apply, whenever the Contract requires that a document or proposed course of action be submitted to the Employer's Representative, the following shall apply:

4.7.1 The Contractor shall give the document or a statement of the proposed action and all necessary supporting information to the Employer's Representative.

4.7.2 The Employer's Representative may [but is not bound to] make a written objection to a Contractor's submission, giving reasons.

4.7.3 The Employer's Representative may request additional information.

4.7.4 The Employer's Representative's period for objection is 10 working days from when the Contractor has given the Employer's Representative enough information to make a purposeful review of the matter submitted should it wish to make one.

4.7.5 The Contractor shall apply in writing for any reduction of the period that it considers desirable in the interests of the Works, which the Employer's Representative may agree if it thinks fit.

4.7.6 The Employer's Representative may alter or withdraw an objection.

4.7.7 The Contractor shall not implement any submission before the period has ended, or contrary to any outstanding objection given within the period.

4.7.8 The Contractor shall make a new submission to meet any objection given within the period.

4.7.9 The Contractor shall also make new submissions as necessary to perform its duties under the Contract [whether or not it has received any objection], and in particular so that its submitted programme shows actual and current planned progress.

4.7.10 The Employer's Representative may object on the grounds that to proceed according to the submission

  (1) would not comply with the Contract or

  (2) would have an adverse effect on the Employer or the public interest or

  (3) would impose an obligation on the Employer that the Contract does not require the Employer to bear or

  (4) would be contrary to a Legal Requirement or

  (5) would have an adverse effect on the Contractor's ability to comply with the Contract

  or any other ground stated in the Contract.

4.7.11 Neither the Employer's Representative's rights to object, nor objections or their absence, reduce any of the Employer's Representative's other powers, or reduce any of the Contractor's responsibilities.

NOTE

The Contract may require the Contractor to provide a document(s) or a proposed course of action to the Employer's Representative. If required, the Contractor shall provide a statement of the proposed action and all supporting information to the Employer's Representative. The Employer's Representative may object to the submission giving reasons. The Employer's Representative may request additional information. The Employer's Representative has 10 working days from when Contractor has provided *enough* information to object to the submission. How the words "enough information" are satisfied is a matter for the Employer's Representative. The Contractor can request a reduction in the time for review and the Employer's Representative may or may not agree as he thinks fit. New submissions may be necessary from the Contractor and the Contractor is obliged to produce these documents. In planning the programme such time periods must be allowed by the Contractor for such approvals and the timing for submissions and approvals needs to be identified clearly on the current programme.

4.8   Value Engineering

4.8.1 The Contractor may give to the Employer's Representative a written value engineering proposal that will, if adopted, either

  (1) reduce the Contract Sum or

  (2) accelerate the execution of the Works, or otherwise be of benefit to the Employer, with no increase to the Contract Sum.

4.8.2 The Contractor's proposal shall include all of the following:

(1) any proposed changes to the Contract

(2) any proposed changes to the Contractor's Documents

(3) a detailed breakdown of the Contractor's original tender cost for the relevant work and the projected cost of the proposal and any proposed adjustment to the Contract Sum to reflect a share of any saving

(4) details of any proposed changes to the programme.

4.8.3 The Employer's Representative shall, as soon as practicable, notify the Contractor whether the Employer agrees to or rejects the proposal. If the Employer agrees to the proposal, the Employer's Representative shall, if agreed, determine a reduction to the Contract Sum and an adjustment to the Date for Substantial Completion of the Works and any affected Section in accordance with the agreed proposal and the Contractor shall implement the agreed proposal. If the proposal is rejected, this shall be conclusive.

4.8.4 If the proposal includes a change in the design of the Works, unless otherwise agreed, the Contractor shall undertake and be liable to the Employer for that design.

NOTE

If the Contractor proposes any value engineering in order to reduce the Contract Sum or accelerate the programme the proposal must provide details of:

(i) The proposed changes to the Contract;

(ii) Proposed changes to the Contractor's Documents;

(iii) A detailed breakdown of the Contractor's original tender cost for the relevant work and the projected cost of the proposal and any proposed adjustment to the Contract Sum to reflect the saving; and

(iv) Details of the proposed changes to the programme.

A submission of this sort will require a great deal of administration. If a Contractor wishes to accelerate the programme he should have all subcontractors and suppliers in full agreement, otherwise subcontractors and suppliers would be committed to a programme that was superseded without their agreement.

If the Employer agrees to the Contractor's value engineering proposal, the saving to the Contract Sum will be determined by the Employer's Representative.

If there is a design element in the proposal then the Contractor is responsible for the design and the cost. This could have implications on insurance and the performance bond.

If a Contractor's value engineering proposal is rejected, such rejection is conclusive.

4.9 Programme

4.9.1 Before the Starting Date, the Contractor shall submit to the Employer's Representative a detailed programme. If there is a programme in the Works Proposals that complies with the Contract, the Contractor shall submit that programme, with any required additional information [such as the actual programmed dates]. The programme shall be of a quality that will permit effective monitoring of the Works and shall, except to the extent that the Works Requirements say or the Employer's Representative agrees that anything may be omitted, include details of all of the following:

(1) when the Contractor will require any instructions, Works Items or other things to be given by the Employer, or anything else the Contract requires the Employer, the Employer's Representative or others to give the Contractor

(2) the order in which and times at which the Contractor proposes to execute the Works, including details of procurement, manufacture, delivery, installation, construction, testing, commissioning and trial operation of Works Items and the sequencing and timing of inspections and of tests

(3) when Contractor's Documents will be submitted to the Employer's Representative

(4) the methods by which the Contractor proposes to execute the Works and any temporary works

(5) the Contractor's estimate of each category of Contractor's Personnel and Contractor's Things expected to be on Site for each period

(6) work to be carried out at the Site by Employer's Personnel and others as provided in the Works Requirements

(7) current critical path, critical resources, floats and other flexibility

(8) details of last review made of programme logic and durations, and of the purposes of any changes

(9) anything else required by the Works Requirements.

4.9.2 The Contractor's programme shall allow reasonable periods of time for the Employer and the Employer's Personnel to comply with their obligations under the Contract.

4.9.3 If the Contractor's programme most recently submitted to the Employer's Representative does not correspond with actual or reasonably projected progress or the Contractor's obligations, the Contractor shall, if so directed by the Employer's Representative, submit to the Employer's Representative a revised programme that complies with this sub-clause and the other provisions of the Contract, showing actual progress and progress projected by the Contractor. If the Contractor asserts that it is not possible to reach Substantial Completion of the Works or a Section by its Date for Substantial Completion, the revised programme shall show Substantial Completion by the earliest possible date. [Neither the programme nor its review will limit the Contractor's responsibility or liability for the delay.] If the Contractor fails to submit the revised programme within 15 working days of a request from the Employer's Representative, the Employer shall be entitled to withhold from the Contractor 15% of any payment to be made to the Contractor until the revised programme is submitted.

> **NOTE**
>
> The programme will be a key document under this Contract. Simple bar charts are unlikely to satisfy the new Contract requirements. An agreed computer software will be necessary as critical paths, critical resources, floats, flexibility, resources, procurement, commissioning details are now required to be incorporated into the programme. The programme will be a fundamental monitoring tool of the progress of the Works. The programme will be the primary document for the assessment of entitlements arising from Delay and Compensation Events.
>
> Contractors should note that if the Contractor fails to provide a revised programme within 15 working days of a request from the Employer's Representative, then the Employer may withhold 15 percent of the value of any payment due to the Contractor until the new programme is provided.

4.10   Progress Reports

4.10.1 The Contractor shall give the Employer's Representative monthly progress reports from the Starting Date until the Contractor has completed all work outstanding on Substantial Completion of the Works. The first report shall cover the period from the Starting Date up to the end of the month in which it occurs, and each subsequent report shall cover one month. The Contractor shall give each progress report within 7 days after the end of the month it relates to. Each progress report shall be in a form agreed by the Employer's Representative.

4.10.2 Each progress report shall include all of the following, except to the extent that the Works Requirements say or the Employer's Representative agrees that any of the following may be omitted:

(1) a detailed description of progress of each stage of the Works against the Contractor's current programme

(2) the names of Specialists and the off-site suppliers of the main Works Items, and progress and location of the design, manufacture, fabrication, delivery, installation, testing and commissioning of Works Items

(3) details of the Contractor's Personnel and Contractor's Things on the Site

(4) status of preparation and review of Contractor's Documents

(5) copies of quality assurance documents and test results and certificates

(6) details of when any instructions to be given by the Employer's Representative will be required, and any that are outstanding

(7) details of when any Works Items or other things to be given by the Employer will be required, and any that are outstanding

(8) details of any Delay Events and Compensation Events that have occurred during the period, or are unresolved

(9) details of any accidents, injuries, hazardous incidents, environmental incidents, labour relations problems and public relations problems concerning or affecting the Works

(10) details of anything that might have an adverse effect on the execution of the Works, the steps the Contractor is taking or proposes to take to reduce those risks, and any steps that the Contractor proposes that the Employer or the Employer's Personnel take to reduce those risks

(11) anything else that the Contractor considers relevant to a progress report

(12) anything else relevant to a progress report that the Employer's Representative directs.

NOTE

Progress reports are, like the programme, elevated to Contract condition status. Within seven days after the end of each month the Contractor shall provide a progress report which shall include the details as outlined above.

4.11   Notice and time for Employer's obligations

4.11.1 The Contractor shall give the Employer's Representative at least 10 working days advance notice of the date by which the Contractor requires any instructions that the Employer's Representative is to give, or Works Items or other things that the Employer is to give.

4.11.2 The latest date for the Employer's Representative to give required instructions, or the Employer to give the Contractor any required Works Item or other thing, shall be the latest of the following:

(1) the date stated in the Contract, if any

(2) the date shown in the Contractor's current programme

(3) the date for which the Contractor first notifies the Employer's Representative under this sub-clause that it is required

(4) the date the Contractor requires the instruction, Works Item or other thing in accordance with its actual progress.

NOTE

The Contractor must provide 10 days advance notice of the date by which instructions are required from the Employer's Representative for work items or other things that the Employer is to provide. This information can be developed when producing the programme. A separate letter with a request for information should also be sent to the Employer's Representative. Any failure by the Employer's

Representative to provide the requested information on time may entitle the Contractor to an extension of time and costs in accordance with Item 7 of Section K of Part 1 of the Schedule.

4.12 Documents

The Contractor shall keep on the Site all of the following:

(1) a full up-to-date set of the Contract documents (but the Pricing Document may be unpriced), instructions of the Employer's Representative, and Contractor's Documents

(2) a log of all instructions and Contractor's Documents showing dates of issue for each and any subsequent revisions

(3) if requested by the Employer's Representative, all publications named in the Contract and the Contractor's Documents.

The Employer's Representative, and any person authorised by the Employer's Representative, shall have the right of access to these at all reasonable times.

NOTE

The Contractor is obliged to keep a copy of all documents including documents referred to in the Contract with the exception of the Contractor's prices. All documents can be accessed by the Employer's Representative or any person authorized by the Employer's Representative.

4.13 Contractor's Management

4.13.1 The Contractor's business includes expertise and experience in construction management.

4.13.2 The Works Proposals include details of the Contractor's initial management arrangements for performing its Contract responsibilities.

4.13.3 The Contractor shall implement the arrangements, and shall add to and otherwise change them, as desirable for its efficient performance.

4.13.4 The arrangements shall include systems, methods, planning and other preparations for providing personnel and resources, programming, recording, consultation, co-ordination, and co-operation, and for flexibility, as referred to in the Contract.

4.13.5 The Contractor shall keep the Employer's Representative fully informed about its current arrangements, in advance, and about their implementation.

4.13.6 The Contractor shall give the Employer's Representative all information, documents and records in the possession of, or available to, the Contractor or the Contractor's Personnel, that the Employer's Representative requires to perform its functions and powers under the Contract.

NOTE

The Contractor must keep the Employer's Representative fully informed about all arrangements for the Works and provide the Employer's Representative with all the documents that he may need to carry out his function under the Contract.

4.14 Communications

4.14.1 The parties intend all communications between them to be interpreted purposefully, having regard to the Contract's purposes.

4.14.2 Whenever any communication [including a notice, decision, objection, approval, certificate, determination, instruction or request] is to be given under the Contract it shall, unless the Contract provides otherwise, be in English, in writing and delivered as follows:

  (1) for notices under clause 12 or clause 13, delivered by hand or sent by pre-paid registered post to the address for those notices in the Schedule, part 1A, as updated by the relevant party

  (2) for other communications, delivered by hand or sent by pre-paid post, fax or email according to the particulars for other communications in the Schedule, part 1A, as updated by the relevant party.

4.14.3 Communications by pre-paid registered post are presumed to have been received at 10:00 hours 2 working days after posting. Fax and email communications are presumed to have been received when receipt is electronically recorded.

NOTE

All communications under the Contract must be in writing and delivered as follows:

  (i) Clause 12 (Termination) and 13 (Disputes) must be delivered/sent by registered post to the address given in Part 1A of the Schedule.

  (ii) Other communications must be delivered, posted, faxed or e-mailed to the relevant party according to the details in Part 1A of the Schedule.

Postal communications are presumed delivered at 10.00 hours, two working days after posting. This is important for ensuring compliance with the strict timetables set down in clauses 9 (Time and Completion) and 10 (Claims and Adjustments). Faxes or e-mails are presumed received when receipt is electronically recorded.

4.15   Meetings

4.15.1 The Contractor's representative and the Employer's Representative shall attend regular meetings scheduled by the Employer's Representative and any special meeting called by either of them to discuss a particular issue identified when calling the meeting. The Employer's Representative may invite other Employer's Personnel and the Contractor may invite Contractor's Personnel to attend meetings. The Contractor shall arrange for the attendance at a meeting of any Contractor's Personnel requested by the Employer's Representative. The time and place of meetings shall be set by the Employer's Representative, after consulting the Contractor, acting reasonably.

4.15.2 Within 5 working days after each meeting the Employer's Representative shall issue minutes of the meeting to the Employer and the Contractor. The Contractor shall notify the Employer's Representative of any objection to the minutes within 5 working days of receiving them, otherwise, unless clearly wrong, they shall be considered correct.

NOTE

Regular meetings shall take place between the Contractor and the Employer's Representative. Special meetings may be called and Employer's Personnel may be requested to attend. The Employer's Representative will issue the minutes within five working days of the meeting. The Contractor then has five working days to object to any minute, and otherwise unless clearly wrong, the minutes are considered correct.

4.16   Confidentiality and Secrecy

4.16.1 The Contractor shall [and shall ensure that the Contractor's Personnel shall] keep confidential:

(1) official information as defined in the Official Secrets Act 1963 and

(2) other information stated in the Works Requirements to be confidential or secret, or that the Employer or the Employer's Representative notifies the Contractor is confidential or secret.

4.16.2 The Employer shall keep confidential the Contractor's rates and prices in the Pricing Document or provided in accordance with the Contract, and any records given by the Contractor under the Contract that the Contractor notifies the Employer's Representative are confidential.

4.16.3 This sub-clause 4.16 shall not prevent disclosure of information, to the extent permitted by Law

(1) to the Contractor's Personnel, the Employer's Personnel or other professional advisors to the Contractor or Employer, who have first entered an undertaking in the terms of this sub-clause 4.16, to the extent necessary for the execution of the Works or to enforce the Contract or

(2) when required by Law or order of a court or, in the case of disclosure by the Employer, for governmental, parliamentary, statutory, administrative, fiscal or judicial purposes, or the publication of an award notice or

(3) that has, except as a result of breach of confidentiality, become available or generally known to the public at the time of the disclosure.

4.16.4 The Contractor's obligations under this sub-clause 4.16 shall be perpetual. The Employer's obligations under this sub-clause shall expire when the commercial sensitivity of the relevant information has ceased, in any event 5 years after the information was given.

> **NOTE**
>
> This is the confidentiality clause. Details of the Contractor's rates and Work Proposals are to be kept confidential by the Employer and the Employer's Representative. This sub-clause shall not prevent disclosure permitted by law, to enable Contractor to complete the Contract. The Contractor's obligation is perpetual. The Employer's obligation is limited to five years.

4.17 Contractor's Things Not to be Removed

The Contractor shall submit details to the Employer's Representative before removing any Contractor's Things from the Site before the Employer's Representative issues a certificate of Substantial Completion of the Works or relevant Section.

> **NOTE**
>
> The Contractor must inform the Employer's Representative before he removes any of the Contractor's Things from site before the Employer's Representative issues a Certificate of Substantial Completion. Contractor's Things are equipment, facilities and other things the Contractor uses to execute the Works, except Works Items. Works Items means a part of the Works or anything the Contractor intends will become art of the Works and temporary works for the Works.

4.18 Contractor's Documents

All Contractor's Documents shall be in English, except when the Works Requirements or the Law specify another language.

> **NOTE**
>
> Clause 4 sets out the manner in which this Contract will be managed and administered. The Contractor must appreciate the substantial management burden imposed on him by this Contract. Effective management and administration is essential and must be compliant with the requirements expressed under clause 4.

5 CONTRACTOR'S PERSONNEL

5.1 Contractor's Personnel to Carry Out Contractor's Obligations

The Contractor is liable for the acts and omissions of Contractor's Personnel [including Specialists and any design they do] as if they were the Contractor's acts and omissions.

5.2 Qualifications and Competence

The Contractor shall ensure that the Contractor's Personnel are suitably qualified and experienced and are competent to carry out their respective tasks.

5.3 Pay and Conditions of Employment

5.3.1 The Contractor shall prominently exhibit copies of this sub-clause 5.3 for the information of persons at the Site. In this sub-clause 5.3 **work person** means an individual employed by, or otherwise working for, the Contractor or the Contractor's Personnel on or adjacent to the Site.

5.3.2 The Contractor shall ensure that the rates of pay and the conditions of employment [including in relation to pension contributions] of each work person comply with all applicable Law, and that those rates and conditions are no less favourable than those for the relevant category of work person in any employment agreements registered under the Industrial Relations Acts 1946 to 2004. The obligations in this sub-clause 5.3 apply regardless of what rates the Contractor has tendered for adjustments to the Contract Sum.

5.3.3 The Contractor shall in respect of

(i) work persons employed by, or otherwise working for, the Contractor and

(ii) all other work persons, ensure that their employers, or the persons for whom they are working,

do all of the following:

(1) pay all wages and other money due to each work person

(2) ensure that work persons' wages are paid in accordance with the Payment of Wages Act 1991 and are never more than 1 month in arrears or unpaid

(3) pay all pension contributions and other amounts due to be paid on behalf of each work person

(4) make all deductions from payments to work persons required by Law, and pay them on as required by Law

(5) keep proper records [including time sheets, wage books and copies of pay slips] showing the wages and other sums paid to and the time worked by each work person, deductions from each work person's pay and their disposition, and pension and other contributions made in respect of each work person, and produce these records for inspection and copying by any persons authorised by the Employer, whenever required by the Employer

(6) produce any other records relating to the rates of pay, pension and other contributions, deductions from pay and their disposition, conditions of employment of work persons, rest periods, and annual leave for inspection and copying by any persons authorised by the Employer, whenever required by the Employer

(7) respect the right under law of work persons to be members of trade unions

(8) observe, in relation to the employment of work persons on the Site, the Safety, Health and Welfare at Work Act, 2005 and all employment law including the Employment

Equality Act 1998, the Industrial Relations Acts 1946 to 2004, the National Minimum Wage Act 2000, and regulations, codes of practice, legally binding determinations of the Labour Court and registered employment agreements under those Laws.

5.3.3A

(1) Sub-clause 5.3.3A(2) shall only be included in the Contract if the Schedule, part 1J says so, and if not, neither sub-clause 5.3.3A(2) nor its omission shall be taken into account.

(2) The Employer shall be entitled to make random checks requiring production of records under sub-clauses 5.3.3(5) and (6).

5.3.4 If the Employer so requests, the Contractor shall, within 5 working days after the receipt of the request, give to the Employer a statement showing the amount of wages and other payments due at the date of the request to and in respect of each work person, or, in respect of work persons not employed by or otherwise working for the Contractor, ensure that their employer or the person for whom they are working does the same.

5.3.5 The Employer may seek information under sub-clause 5.3.3 only for the purpose of ensuring the obligations referred to in this sub-clause 5.3 to work persons have been properly discharged. All information given under sub-clause 5.3.3 shall be returned to the person providing them or destroyed if the Employer is satisfied that the relevant employer has complied with legal obligations to work persons.

5.3.6 If the Contractor has not complied with this sub-clause 5.3, the Employer shall [without limiting its other rights or remedies] be entitled to estimate the amount that should have been paid to work persons and contributions that should have been made on their behalf, and the Employer may deduct the estimated amount from any payment due to the Contractor, until the Employer is satisfied that all proper amounts have been paid.

5.3.7 The Contractor shall give the Employer's Representative with each interim statement under sub-clause 11.1 a certificate in the form in the Works Requirements, that, in respect of the work to which the interim certificate relates, the Contractor has complied in full with this sub-clause 5.3.

5.3.8 If the Contractor does not comply with this sub-clause 5.3, it shall pay to the Employer any costs the Employer incurs in investigating and dealing with the non-compliance.

NOTE

The Contractor shall ensure that the rates of pay and conditions of employment of each work person comply with applicable law and are no less favourable than those for the relevant category of work person in any employment agreement registered under the Industrial Relations Acts 1946–2004. The Contractor is also responsible for the compliance of subcontractors, including labour hire, with this condition. The Contractor is responsible for the enforcement of these requirements and any breach can be grounds for termination.

To confirm the Contractor's compliance with Condition 5.3, Condition 5.3.7 requires the Contractor to provide the Employer's Representative with a certificate (in the form in the Works Requirements) that the Contractor has complied in full with sub-clause 5.3. This certificate has to be submitted with each interim statement submitted by the Contractor under sub-clause 11.1 (Interim Payment); otherwise there will be no payment for the relevant Work Item until the certificate is given. This requirement is of particular importance for contractors as non compliance will incur financial penalties and is a ground for termination by the employer under clause 12.1.1.9.

5.4 Subcontractors and Specialists

5.4.1 The Contractor shall not subcontract all of the Works to one or more Subcontractors. If the Contractor intends to subcontract part of the Works, other than when the Subcontractor and its scope are set out in the Contract, or the Contract provides other procedures, the Contractor shall first submit details to the Employer's Representative of the proposed Subcontractor and its proposed scope of work. The Contractor shall also submit details to the Employer's Representative of any proposed Specialist, other than one named in the Contract or when the Contract provides other procedures.

> **NOTE**
>
> The Contract allows for Named Subcontractors (Specialists). All Subcontractors will be engaged on a domestic basis. The Contractor has to obtain the acceptance of the Employer's Representative to any proposed Specialist. Clause 4.10 (Progress Reports).2 (2) also requires all Subcontractors/ Specialists to be listed in the Progress Reports.

5.4.2   If Specialists or other Contractor's Personnel are named in the Contract, the Contractor shall ensure that they are engaged for and perform the work for which they are named.

> **NOTE**
>
> If the Specialist or other Contractor's personnel are named in the Employer's Work Requirements the Contractor shall ensure that they are engaged for the Works set out and named in the Contract.
> The following pretender procedures will apply:
>
> • The tender for the specialist work will be completed before the competition for the main Contract;
>
> • The name of the Specialist, the subcontract price and the subcontract agreement will be included in the Works Requirements issued to tender.
>
> The Employer should obtain an undertaking from the Specialist that he will enter into a subcontract with the Contractor on terms and obligations that apply under the main Contract. There is no right of objection from the Contractor as the Specialist is named in the tender document which he cannot alter and is therefore part of his bid.

5.4.3   If the Works Requirements name a Specialist whose contract with the Employer is to be novated to the Contractor, and include a copy of that contract, the Contractor shall accept the novation, and the parties shall, at the same time as entering the Agreement, enter the novation agreement in the Works Requirements.

> **NOTE**
>
> If the Work Requirements name a Specialist whose Contract is to be novated to the Contractor and includes a copy of the Contract, the Contractor shall accept the novation and execute the novation agreement at the same time as the main Contract is executed. The process at tender stage is similar to 5.4.2 above. The Employer's Representative may not instruct the Contractor to enter into a subcontract with the Specialist selected by the Employer's Representative unless that Specialist was named in the Contract.

5.4.4   The Employer's Representative may not instruct the Contractor to enter a contract with a particular Specialist selected by the Employer's Representative unless the Specialist is named in the Contract.

5.4.5   The Contractor shall fully comply with its obligations under any contract with a Specialist and shall not terminate, allow to be terminated or accept a repudiation of such a contract without first submitting details to the Employer's Representative, except when an insolvency event, as set out in sub-clause 12.1, occurs in respect of the Specialist, or the Specialist has committed a serious breach of Law concerning safety, or the Specialist has failed to put or keep in effect insurance as required by the Specialist's contract. On any termination, the Contractor shall replace the Specialist, having submitted details of the replacement to the Employer's Representative.

5.4.6 In addition to the reasons in sub-clause 4.7, the Employer's Representative may object to the proposed replacement of Contractor's Personnel because the proposed replacement does not have at least the level of experience, qualifications, competence, technical capacity, and financial standing of the person being replaced.

5.5 Collateral Warranties

If the Schedule, part 1F, states that a collateral warranty is required from any Specialist, before the date stated in the Schedule, the Contractor shall give the Employer a collateral warranty in the form included in the Works Requirements, or if there is none, a form approved by the Employer, executed by the Specialist and the Contractor.

5.6 Removal of Work Persons

The Contractor shall remove from the Site any Contractor's Personnel that the Employer's Representative directs, because of the Contractor's Personnel's negligence or incompetence, or on the basis that the Contractor's Personnel's presence on the Site is not conducive to safety, health or good order.

6   PROPERTY

6.1   Ownership of Works Items

It is agreed, and the Contractor shall ensure, that each Works Item shall become the property of the Employer on the earliest of the following:

    (1)   when it is delivered to the Site, if owned by the Contractor

    (2)   when it is incorporated in the Works

    (3)   when any payment for the Works Item is made by the Employer to the Contractor.

> **NOTE**
>
> This sub-clause deals with ownership of Work Items and is particularly relevant to situations of insolvency. The Contractor is to ensure property passes to Employer when it is delivered to the site if owned by the Contractor. Work Items means a part of the Works, or anything that the Contractor intends will become part of the Works and temporary works for the Works.

6.2   Infringement of Property Rights

6.2.1   The Contractor shall indemnify the Employer against any liability resulting from any of the following infringing the property [including intellectual property] rights of any person:

    (1)   the Contractor's performance or non-performance of this Contract, unless the liability is covered by the Employer's indemnity in this sub-clause

    (2)   use of Works Items, Contractor's Things, or Contractor's Documents by

        (a)   the Contractor or Contractor's Personnel or

        (b)   the Employer or any other person to complete the Works following termination of the Contractor's obligation to complete the Works

    (3)   use by the Employer of the Works, Works Items, or the Contractor's Documents for the purpose for which they were given.

6.2.2   The Employer shall indemnify the Contractor against any liability resulting from any of the following infringing the property [including intellectual property] rights of any person:

    (1)   the unavoidable use by the Contractor, in accordance with the Contract, of the Works Requirements or Works Items or other things provided by the Employer

    (2)   the use or occupation by the Works of the parts of the Site described in the Works Requirements as lands made available by the Employer for the Works, when that is the unavoidable result of performing the Contract.

> **NOTE**
>
> Sub-clause 6.2 deals with indemnifying the Employer from infringement of property rights, including intellectual rights.

6.3   Works Requirements

The Works Requirements shall remain the property of the Employer and the Contractor shall not use them [and shall ensure that the Contractor's Personnel do not use them] for any purpose other than to perform the Contract or to prosecute or defend a dispute under the Contract.

6.4   Property and Rights in Contractor's Documents

6.4.1   The Employer may use, copy, modify, adapt and translate for any purpose in connection with the Works [including to construct, maintain, extend, use, operate, let, sell, promote, advertise, reinstate and repair the Works] the Contractor's Documents that are given, or, according to the Contract, must be given, to the Employer and the Works Proposals.

6.4.2   If the Schedule, part 1C, so states, ownership of and all copyright and other rights in the Contractor's Documents that are prepared for the Works and are given, or according to the Contract, must be given, to the Employer and the Works Proposals transfers to the Employer when the Employer receives them.

6.4.3   The Contractor shall ensure that the Employer obtains the rights and interests described in this sub-clause 6.4.

6.4.4   The Contractor has no liability for the use of the Contractor's Documents for any purpose other than that for which they were given to the Employer.

NOTE

Sub-clause 6.4 deals with the property and rights in the Contractor's Documents, which the Employer has the right to use, copy, modify, adopt or translate for any purpose in connection with the Works. Part 1C of the Schedule may state that handover of copyright to the Employer and the Contractor shall ensure that all those rights can be transferred, including copyright to documents provided by Contractor's Personnel. The Contractor is not liable for the use of the Contractor's Documents for any purpose other than that for which they were provided to the Employer.

GENERAL NOTES ON CLAUSE 6

This clause deals with Property Rights associated with the Works. The Employer is concerned to ensure that he will receive clear title to anything which will be incorporated into his building, and in this regard the Contractor is required to obtain clear title to items to be incorporated into the Works.

This clause provides that the Employer retains ownership of the Works Requirements, whilst he must *obtain* ownership of the Contractor's Documents should the Employer wish to exercise this option.

7   THE SITE

7.1   Lands Made Available for the Works

7.1.1   The Employer shall allow the Contractor to occupy and use each part of the Site described in the Works Requirements as lands made available by the Employer for the Works from a date on or before the latest of the following:

(1)   the Starting Date

(2)   the day after the Contractor has done what sub-clause 9.1 requires the Contractor to do before the Starting Date

(3)   the date stated in the Works Requirements, if any

(4)   the day after the Contractor has submitted its programme according to sub-clause 4.9

(5)   the date stated for work to start on the part of the Site in the Contractor's current programme

(6)   the date the Contractor actually requires the part in accordance with its actual progress.

7.1.2   The Contractor's right to occupy and use the Site shall be subject to any limitations in the Works Requirements.

> **NOTE**
>
> The possession and access to the site will be subject to limitations as expressed in the Work Requirements.

7.1.3   The Contractor shall not be entitled to exclusive possession of the Site or any part of it and shall facilitate any occupation and use of the Site by the Employer and others stated in the Works Requirements. The Contractor's right to occupy and use the Site shall be solely for the purpose of performing the Contract.

7.1.4   The Contractor's right to occupy and use the Site shall end when the Employer's Representative certifies the Works or the relevant Section as Substantially Complete. After then the Employer shall allow the Contractor access to comply with sub-clause 8.6.1.

7.1.5   The Contractor's right to occupy and use a part of the Site shall end if the Employer takes over the relevant part of the Works under sub-clause 9.7.

7.1.6   The Contractor's right to occupy and use the Site shall end if the Contractor's obligation to complete the Works is terminated.

> **NOTE**
>
> The Employer shall allow access to the site on or before the latest of the following dates:
>
> (i)   The Starting Date – which is the date the Contractor proposes to start executing the Works on site, as notified by the Contractor to the Employer's Representative.
>
> (ii) The day after the Contractor has done what sub-clause 9.1 (Starting Date) requires the Contractor to do before the Starting Date. This includes to:
>
> > (a)   Execute the Agreement;
> >
> > (b)   Provide the performance bond;
> >
> > (c)   Provide the parent company guarantee;

(d) If it is required by the Contract execute the appointment of the Contractor as Project Supervisor;

(e) Provide evidence that all insurances are in place;

(f) Provide any Collateral Warranties (these may be supplied later with the agreement of the Employer's Representative).

(iii) The date stated in the Works Requirement.

(iv) The day after the Contractor has submitted its programme in accordance with sub-clause 4.9.

(v) The day stated for work to start on part of the site in the Contractor's current programme.

(vi) The date the Contractor actually requires the part in accordance with its actual programme.

The Contractor must insure all the Contract requirements are in place in advance of the Starting Date, otherwise the Employer does not have to give access to the site.

By sub-clause 7.1.3 the Contractor is not entitled to exclusive possession of the site.

7.2   Trespassers

After the Employer has allowed the Contractor to occupy and use the Site, the Contractor shall be responsible for activities of trespassers, protesters and others, that are not Employer's Personnel, on the Site, and the Employer shall have no responsibility to the Contractor for their activities or presence.

NOTE

The Contractor is responsible for trespassers and the Employer shall have no responsibility to the Contractor for their activities or presence. The Contractor will have to study the Work Requirements to establish if any parts of the site or facilities have to be operated and maintained during the course of the Works. Any costs involved will have to be built into the tender. In the event that facilities have to be operated the full extent of such should be determined as it could have serious implications on cost and resources.

7.3   Contractor Responsible for all Site Operations

The Contractor shall be responsible for all operations on the Site connected with the execution of the Works.

7.4   Services for Employer's Facilities

The Contractor shall operate and maintain parts of the Site and facilities of the Employer if the Works Requirements so require.

NOTE

The extent of what is meant by "operate and maintain" is new and would need to be carefully checked from the Work Requirements. Operate is not usually a "Contractor" function so this could be a serious resource and cost issue.

7.5   Security and Safety of the Site and Nuisance

7.5.1   From and including the Starting Date until the Employer's Representative certifies the Works or the relevant Section as Substantially Complete, or the Employer takes over the relevant part of the Works under sub-clause 9.7, the Contractor shall do all of the following [without limiting other obligations]:

(1) be responsible for securing the Site and for keeping off the Site persons other than any of the following:

    (i) the Contractor's Personnel and the Employer's Personnel

    (ii) any other person notified to the Contractor by the Employer or the Employer's Representative as authorised to enter the Site

    (iii) persons exercising public access to any roads, footpaths and areas on the Site

    (iv) persons having a right to enter the Site under Legal Requirements

(2) keep the Site in good order and free from unnecessary obstructions

(3) take all necessary steps to secure the safety of all persons entitled to be on the Site and to protect users, owners and occupiers of land adjacent to the Site from hazards and interference arising from the Works [including providing any required fences, lighting, guarding, watching, roads and footpaths]

(4) take all necessary steps to ensure that the Contractor, the Contractor's Personnel and the execution of the Works do not do any of the following:

    (i) unnecessarily cause a nuisance or inconvenience to the public or any user, owner or occupier of any land, road or footpath on or adjacent to the Site

    (ii) unnecessarily interfere with the use of any such land, road or footpath.

7.5.2 The Employer shall ensure that Employer's Personnel on the Site comply with the Contractor's reasonable safety rules that have been notified to them by the Contractor.

NOTE

This sub-clause deals with security and safety of site and nuisance, which are normal Contractor responsibilities. The Contractor has to permit the public to continue to exercise their right of public access to roads, footpaths and areas on the site.

7.6   Other Contractors

Where so stated in the Works Requirements, the Employer may arrange for work to be executed on the Site by Employer's Personnel. The Contractor shall co-operate with such Employer's Personnel and shall as far as practicable co-ordinate their activities with the execution of the Works.

NOTE

The Contractor has to allow access to the Employer's Personnel which are the Employer's Representative, the Employer's Employees, agents and consultants, other contractors of the Employer working on the site when acting within the scope of their contracts with the Employer, and, finally, anyone else the Employer's Representative advises the Contractor is an Employer's Personnel.

7.7   Setting Out the Works

The Contractor shall set out the Works by reference to the points, lines and levels of reference in the Works Requirements. The Contractor shall be responsible for the correct positioning of all parts of the Works and shall rectify any errors in the positions, levels, dimensions or alignment of the Works. Before setting out the Works the Contractor shall make all reasonable efforts to verify the accuracy of the setting out information in the Works Requirements.

7.8   Archaeological Objects and Human Remains

If any fossils, coins, antiquities, monuments or other items of value or of archaeological or geological interest or human remains are discovered on or adjacent to the Site, the Contractor shall not disturb them, but shall take all necessary steps to preserve them, and shall promptly notify the Employer's Representative [and comply with any instructions]. As between the parties, these items shall be the Employer's property.

7.9   Access and Facilities

7.9.1   The Contractor [and not the Employer] shall be responsible for the suitability and availability of access routes to and within the Site, and any required maintenance or upgrading of them, and any charges for use of them.

7.9.2   The Contractor shall take all reasonable steps to ensure that its traffic [including Contractor's Personnel's traffic]

(1)   complies with the restrictions concerning laden weight and dimensions in the Law and

(2)   does not damage roads [except for ordinary wear], bridges or other property.

7.9.3   The Contractor shall also be responsible for obtaining any additional facilities, and for providing all power, water and other services it requires to perform the Contract.

7.10   Condition of Site on Completion

As soon as practicable after the Works or any Section reaches Substantial Completion, the Contractor shall remove from the Site Contractor's Things not required to perform the Contractor's remaining obligations, and leave the Works or Section in an orderly manner. At the end of the Defects Period, the Contractor shall remove from the Site any remaining Contractor's Things. In this sub-clause 7.10, Contractor's Things includes temporary works that have not become part of the Works.

7.11   Working Times

The Contractor shall ensure that the Contractor's Personnel work on the Site only during the working times set out in the Works Requirements, if any, unless

(1)   there is imminent danger to safety or health or of damage to the Works or other property or

(2)   otherwise agreed with the Employer's Representative.

NOTE

This sub-clause makes it a condition to keep within legal working hours as set down in planning Consents or other documents where they are set out in Work Requirements, unless there is imminent danger to health and safety or damage to Works or to property or it is otherwise agreed with the Employer's Representative.

GENERAL NOTES ON CLAUSE 7

This clause sets out the obligations of the Parties in relation to delivery and occupation of the Site. The Employer is required to deliver the Site, or any part of it, to the Contractor by, at the latest, the date upon which the Contractor actually requires the part of the site in accordance with actual progress. The Contractor will not obtain exclusive possession of the Site or any part of it. This clause places the responsibility for trespassers with the Contractor. The only people who will be contractually compelled to abide by the Contractor's safety rules will be the Employer's and Contractor's Personnel.

The Contractor, from the Starting Date becomes entirely responsible for all operations on the Site (Clause 7.5.1), and for safety and security.

The Contractor is responsible for setting out in accordance with the Works Requirements. The Contractor will also be required to take care of archaeological finds, should the Employer so elect under Item 18 of the Schedule, Part 1K.

The Contractor is responsible for access routes, traffic and utilities required for the execution of the Works. On completion of the Works, the Contractor shall remove Contractor's Things from the Site (including Temporary Works). The clause also provides that the Works will only be undertaken during pre-specified Working Times.

7.12   Charges

The Contractor shall pay any charges provided for in the Works Requirements for occupation of the Site or any part of it or other place, or in respect of operation or maintenance of Employer's facilities, or in respect of services, or otherwise. [The Employer may deduct the amount of charges from payment to the Contractor. Payment of charges does not excuse the Contractor from any of its obligations.]

NOTE

Details of the prescribed charges should be detailed in the Works Requirements at tender stage for incorporation into the contractor's tender sum.

8 QUALITY, TESTING AND DEFECTS

8.1 Standards of Workmanship and Works Items

The Contractor shall ensure all of the following:

    (1)   that the Works are executed and completed

        (i)   in accordance with all the requirements in, and reasonably inferred from, the Contract [including, where so required by the Contract, in accordance with Contractor's Documents that have been submitted to the Employer's Representative] and

        (ii)   in a proper and workmanlike manner and using good practice

    (2)   that all Works Items [whether or not the Contractor is required to select them]

        (i)   comply with the Contract and the Legal Requirements and

        (ii)   are of good quality and, unless the Contract provides otherwise, new

    (3)   that all materials and goods that are Works Items [whether or not the Contractor is required to select them] are fit for the purpose for which they are normally used

    (4)   that all Works Items selected or designed by the Contractor [including by any Specialist] are fit for their intended purpose in the Works.

> **NOTE**
>
> All materials and goods are to be new and of good quality unless otherwise provided in the Work Requirements.

8.2 Quality Assurance

The Contractor shall establish and implement quality assurance procedures as required by the Works Requirements, including procedures for establishing quality assurance systems for itself and Subcontractors. The quality assurance procedures shall be reflected in appropriate quality plans submitted to the Employer's Representative. The Contractor shall give the Employer's Representative copies of all reports prepared in accordance with the Contractor's quality assurance procedures. The Employer's Representative may monitor, spot check and audit the Contractor's quality assurance procedures.

> **NOTE**
>
> Sub-clause 8.2 deals with the expected quality assurance procedures that the Contractor shall establish. The Employer's Representative is entitled to a copy of the Contractor's quality assurance plan and all reports prepared by the Contractor. The Employer's Representative is entitled to monitor, audit and spot check the Contractor's quality assurance procedure.

8.3 Inspection

    8.3.1   The Contractor shall ensure that the Employer's Representative, and anyone authorised by the Employer's Representative, is able at all reasonable times to have access to all places where the Works are being executed [whether or not at the Site] and any place where any Works Items are produced, stored, extracted or prepared, or any other obligation of the Contractor under the Contract is being performed, and are able there to inspect, test, observe and examine all such items and activities.

8.3.2   The Contractor shall promptly give the Employer's Representative all particulars the Employer's Representative requests about the mode, place and time of manufacture, the source of supply and the performance capabilities of Works Items and any related information, including any test certificates that the Contract provides for.

8.3.3   The Contractor shall notify the Employer's Representative before any Works Item is covered or any Works Item that is to be inspected is packed or made impossible or difficult to inspect, in either case giving the Employer's Representative, and any person authorised by the Employer's Representative, a reasonable opportunity to inspect the Works Item.

NOTE

The Contractor is to give the Employer's Representative notice of when Work Items that require inspection are being covered up or packaged or made impossible or difficult to inspect. The Contractor shall notify the Employer's Representative and provide a reasonable opportunity for the inspection to take place.

8.4   Tests

8.4.1   The Contractor shall supply all Contractor's Things, documents, information, suitably qualified and experienced personnel, power, consumables and instruments required to carry out tests that the Contract requires the Contractor to do [both before and after Substantial Completion]. The Contractor shall agree with the Employer's Representative the time and place for these tests. The Employer's Representative, and others authorised by the Employer, may attend and observe the tests, and the Contractor shall facilitate their attendance and observation. Regardless of whether any Employer's Personnel attends, the Contractor shall promptly give the Employer's Representative a certified report of the result of every test.

8.4.2   If a test is failed, the Contractor may elect to repeat the test, or the Employer's Representative may require that the test be repeated. The Contractor shall, on request, pay the Employer any costs the Employer incurs as a result of any re-testing.

8.4.3   If the Contractor rectifies a Defect, it shall repeat any relevant test the Contract specifies for the relevant Works Item, if the Employer's Representative so directs.

NOTE

This sub-clause deals with the carrying out of all tests which the Contractor is required by the Contract to do, both before and after Substantial Completion. The Contractor is to facilitate the attendance of the Employer's Representative to observe the tests, and to provide certified reports of result of each test. If a test fails the Contractor may elect to retest or be instructed by the Employer's Representative. The Contractor is responsible for the Employer's costs arising from any retest. If the Contractor repairs a defect for which he is at fault he shall repeat any relevant test to that Work if so requested by the Employer's Representative at the Contractor's cost.

8.5   Defects

8.5.1   The Employer's Representative may direct the Contractor to search for a Defect or suspected Defect or its cause. This may include uncovering, dismantling, re-covering and re-erecting work, providing facilities for tests, testing and inspecting. If, through searching or otherwise, the Contractor discovers a Defect, the Contractor shall notify the Employer's Representative as soon as practicable.

8.5.2   If, through notification or otherwise, the Employer's Representative becomes aware of a Defect, the Employer's Representative may direct the Contractor to do any of the following [or any combination of them]:

(1)   to remove the Works Item with the Defect from the Site

(2)   to demolish the Works Item with the Defect, if incorporated in the Works

(3) to reconstruct, replace or correct the Works Item with the Defect

(4) not to deliver the Works Item with the Defect to the Site.

8.5.3 The Contractor shall comply with any direction under this sub-clause 8.5 within the reasonable times, if any, the Employer's Representative directs. If the Contractor fails to begin the work required to comply with the direction within the reasonable time directed, if any, or to complete it as soon as practicable, the Employer may have the work done by others and the Contractor shall, on request, pay the Employer its cost of doing so.

8.5.4 Alternatively, the Contractor and the Employer's Representative may, with the Employer's consent, agree that the Employer will accept the Defect, either in whole or subject to any change to the Works Requirements that the Employer's Representative directs. In this case, the Contract Sum shall be reduced by the amount that, in the opinion of the Employer's Representative, is the resulting decrease in the value of the Works to the Employer. If the Employer's Representative notifies the Contractor that the Employer will not accept a Defect, this shall be conclusive.

8.5.5 If a Defect deprives the Employer of substantially the whole benefit of the Works or any Section or other material part of the Works, the Employer's Representative may reject the Works or the relevant part of the Works (as the case may be) and [without limiting the Employer's other rights], the Contractor shall pay the Employer all sums the Employer has paid the Contractor for the Works or the relevant part, together with the Employer's financing costs and the cost of dismantling and removing the Works, clearing the Site and returning the Works Items to the Contractor.

8.5.6 The Employer's Representative may give a direction or rejection under this sub-clause 8.5 at any time before the Defects Certificate is issued. [The Contractor shall not be entitled to any adjustment to the Contract Sum or extension of time because of a direction given to deal with, or as a result of, a Defect or any other breach of the Contract by the Contractor.]

NOTE

This sub-clause deals with defects which now includes all workmanship and materials and Contractor's documentation which may not be in accordance with the Contract. In dealing with a defect there are five options open to the Employer's Representative:

(i) Remove the Work Item with defect from the site

(ii) Demolish Work Item with defect if incorporated in Works

(iii) Reconstruct, replace or correct the Works with the defect

(iv) Not deliver the Work Items with the defect to the site

(v) Alternatively, the Employer's Representative and the Contractor, with the Employer's agreement, may accept the defect either in whole or subject to any change in Work Requirements instructed by the Employer's Representative. Any resulting decrease in value of the Works shall be determined by the Employer's Representative and the amount shall be deducted from the Contract Sum. Such deduction may not relate solely to cost alone.

If the Employer's Representative will not accept a defect it shall be conclusive under this Contract.

The Employer's Representative may reject the Works or part of the Works if the defect denies the Employer of, substantially, the whole benefit of the Works or part thereof. The Contractor shall pay the Employer all sums paid to the Contractor by the Employer for those Works or the part of the Works rejected, together with the Employer's financing costs, the cost of dismantling the Works and removing from the site, and the costs of returning Work Items to the Contractor.

No adjustment to cost or time are allowed for a defect which is the fault of the Contractor.

8.6 Defects Period

8.6.1 As soon as practicable after Substantial Completion of the Works or any Section, the Contractor shall complete any outstanding work and rectify any Defects that the Employer's Representative directs before the end of the Defects Period. In doing so, and in doing any tests after Substantial Completion, the Contractor shall cause as little disruption as possible to occupants and users of the Works.

8.6.2 If work remains outstanding or Defects remain uncorrected at the end of the Defects Period, or if the Contractor has completed outstanding work or rectified Defects after Substantial Completion of the Works or relevant Section and before the end of the Defects Period, the Employer's Representative may [without limiting the Employer's other rights] make an appropriate extension to the Defects Period. With the Employer's agreement the Employer's Representative may, at the time that the Defects Period would have ended without this extension, issue an interim payment certificate conclusively making an appropriate reduction in retention, and the Contractor shall be entitled to invoice the Employer for that amount.

> **NOTE**
>
> Sub-clause 8.6 deals with the remedy of defects in the Defects Period. The Employer's Representative may, where serious defects have occurred during the Defects Period, seek to have the period extended to monitor the defects. The Contractor may agree and there will be an appropriate reduction to retention at the original defects completion date.
>
> If no extension is agreed the Employer's Representative may, at the end of Defects Period, assess the risk that defects in the Work Item concerned may occur or be noticed in the period from the remedial work to the Works Item and equal in length to the Defects Period, and make an appropriate deduction to the Contract Sum to compensate the Employer for that risk.
>
> Sub-clause 8.6.2 (Defects Period) entitles the Employer's Representative to reduce the Contract Sum to compensate the Employer against the risk of defects occurring in the future.

8.7 Defects Certificate

The Employer's Representative shall issue the Defects Certificate to the Contractor and the Employer within 20 working days after the end of the Defects Period. [Nothing in this clause 8, nor any exercise or non-exercise by the Employer or the Employer's Representative of their rights under this clause 8, nor the Defects Certificate, relieves the Contractor of any obligation, except to the extent that a Defect is accepted by agreement under sub-clause 8.5.4.]

> **NOTE**
>
> The Defects Certificate means a certificate of the Employer's Representative issued to certify that the Defects Period has ended. The Employer's Representative shall issue this certificate to the Contractor and the Employer within 20 working days after the end of the Defects Period.

> **GENERAL NOTE ON CLAUSE 8**
>
> The Works Requirements will contain quality assurance procedures. The Contractor should establish and implement these requirements. The quality assurance procedures shall be reflected in the appropriate documents that the Contractor submits to the Employer's Representative. The Employer's Representative may monitor, carry out spot checks and audit the Contractor's quality assurance procedures.
>
> The Defects Period means the period starting on Substantial Completion of the Works and continuing for the period stated in the Schedule, Part 1, Section I (which, if none is stated, should taken to be one year) as may be extended under clause 8.6.2.
>
> In the event that the Contractor does not agree with the amount of the reduction to the Contract Sum the Contractor can refer the issue to conciliation under sub-clause 13.1.
>
> Where the Defects Period is extended there will also be issues with the release of the bond and maintaining insurances on the project. The Contractor will have to inform his bondsman and insurance agents.

9 TIME AND COMPLETION

9.1 Starting Date

9.1.1 The Contractor shall set the Starting Date, giving the Employer's Representative at least 15 working days notice, or any shorter period the Employer's Representative may agree, or any different period stated in the Works Requirements. The Starting Date shall, unless otherwise stated in the Works Requirements, be no more than 20 working days after the Contract Date.

9.1.2 Before the Starting Date [unless already given by the Contractor before the Contract Date, for example in response to a letter of intent] the Contractor shall give the Employer all of the following, all executed, as relevant, by the relevant persons:

(1) the Agreement

(2) a performance bond, if required by the Contract

(3) a parent company guarantee, if required by the Contract

(4) if the Works Requirements state that the Contractor or the Contractor's nominee is to be appointed as project supervisor for the construction stage, the required appointment, and the developed safety and health plan required by the Construction Regulations

(5) evidence that the insurances required by the Contract are in effect

(6) any collateral warranties required by the Contract

However, collateral warranties may be given on a later date that the Employer's Representative has agreed to.

9.1.3 On the Starting Date, the Contractor shall start to execute the Works on the Site. The Contractor shall, unless the Employer's Representative directs otherwise, proceed regularly and diligently in order to achieve Substantial Completion of the Works and each Section by its Date for Substantial Completion.

NOTE

Sub clause 9.1 deals with the Starting Date. Notice of 15 working day must be given to the Employer's Representative, or any shorter period agreed or as per the Work Requirements.

Unless it is otherwise stated in the Work Requirements, the Starting Date shall be no later than 20 working days after the Contract Date.

The Contractor must comply with the following obligations before the Starting Date:

(i) Executing the Agreement;

(ii) Providing the performance bond, if required;

(iii) Providing parent company guarantees, if required;

(iv) If required under the Work Requirements, confirming acceptance of the appointment as project supervisor for the construction stage, and providing a copy of the developed health and safety plan;

(v) Providing evidence that the insurances required by the Contract is in place;

(vi) Providing collateral warranties required, though they may be deferred to later date by the Employer's Representative, or as per the Schedule.

(vii) Ensuring that his organisation is prepared and ready to have these documents in place.

It is possible that works could be delayed for want of sufficient time to serve a statutory notice. It may be necessary to work under a Letter of Intent as contained in the Model Forms. The Contractor should ensure that any Letter of Intent provides for the Contractor to be paid for all Works and documents produced in the event that the project is delayed or cancelled.

9.2   Suspension

9.2.1 The Employer's Representative may at any time direct the Contractor to suspend all or part of the work under the Contract. The Contractor shall comply with the direction and, during suspension, shall protect, store and secure the affected Works Items against deterioration, loss and damage and maintain the Insurances.

9.2.2 After a suspension under clause 9.2.1, the Contractor shall resume work when so directed by the Employer's Representative. When a direction to resume is given, the Contractor and the Employer's Representative shall jointly examine the Works and Works Items affected by the suspension. If the Contractor is entitled to an adjustment of the Contract Sum or an extension of time because of the suspension, the Contractor's cost of rectifying any deterioration in or loss of the Works or Work Items that the Contractor could not have avoided shall be included in the determination of the adjustment, and any resulting delay shall be taken into account in determining the extension.

9.2.3 If a suspension, that did not result from a breach of the Contractor's obligations, has continued for more than 3 months, the Contractor may request the Employer's Representative's permission to proceed. If the Employer's Representative does not give permission within 28 days after being requested to do so, the Contractor may, by giving notice to the Employer's Representative

(1) if the suspension affects part of the Works, treat the suspension as a Change Order to omit that part of the Works or

(2) if the suspension affects the whole of the Works, give notice to terminate the Contractor's obligation to complete the Works under the Contract.

> **NOTE**
>
> The Employer may suspend the Works. In the event of a suspension the Works have to be protected, stored and kept secure. The Works will be resumed on instruction from the Employer's Representative. The Contractor is entitled to the cost of any remedial works. The Contractor is entitled to an adjustment of the Contract Sum and an extension of time, both of which have to be assessed.
>
> Suspension under 9.2 is a Delay and Compensation Event (Item 3 of the Schedule, Part 1, Section K). Costs are calculated at the daily delay rate quoted by the Contractor in the Schedule (Part 2, Section E). These costs may not cover the Contractor's full costs, e.g. costs from subcontractors and offsite storage and the like.
>
> If the suspension lasts more than three months then the Contractor may treat the instruction to suspend as an instruction to omit that part of the Works or give notice to terminate the Contractor's obligations under the Contract.

9.3   Delay and Extension of Time

9.3.1 If the Contractor becomes aware that work under the Contract is being or is likely to be delayed for any reason, it shall as soon as practicable notify the Employer's Representative of the delay and its cause. As soon as practicable after that, and in any event within 40 working days after the Contractor became aware of the delay, the Contractor shall give the Employer's Representative full details of the delay and its effect on the progress of the Works. But if the Contractor has given notice and details of the delay under sub-clause 10.3.1 it does not have to give notice or details again under this sub-clause 9.3.1 for the same delay. In any event, the Contractor shall promptly give any further information about the delay the Employer's Representative directs.

> **NOTE**
>
> Sub-clause 9.3 is a critical clause. In order to retain any rights to receive extensions and costs to cover resulting delay, the Contractor's organisation needs to follow it to the letter.

Under sub-clause 9.3.1, where the Contractor is aware that the work is being or is likely to be delayed for any reason, he shall, as soon as is practicable, notify the Employer's Representative of the delay and cause.

Within 40 working days, at the most, after the contractor became aware of the delay he shall give to the Employer's Representative full details of delay and its effect on progress and promptly supply any further information on the delay requested by the Employer's Representative.

Note that this means any delay, not just those to which an entitlement to an extension of time is given. If the contractor has already given notice and details of the delay under sub-clause 10.3.1, the contractor does not have to give notice and details for the same delay under sub-clause 9.3.1.

9.3.2   If Substantial Completion of the Works or any Section has been, is being or will be delayed beyond the Date for Substantial Completion by a Delay Event and if all of the following apply:

(1)   the Delay Event is not a result of the Contractor's or Contractor's Personnel's act or omission or the Contractor's breach of the Contract

(2)   the Contractor cannot avoid the delay and makes all reasonable efforts to minimise the delay

(3)   the Contract does not provide otherwise

then, subject to this sub-clause 9.3, sub-clause 9.4 and clause 10, there shall be an extension to the Date for Substantial Completion of the Works and any affected Section equal to the amount of the delay beyond the Date for Substantial Completion caused by the Delay Event, taking into account only Site Working Days. The Contractor and the Employer's Representative shall follow the procedure in clause 10.

NOTE

Sub-clause 9.3.2.deals with delay to the Substantial Completion Date of whole or part of the Works which has been, is being or will be affected. The delays must not be the result of an act, omission or breach of Contract by the Contractor. The Delay Event must be one that could not be avoided. The Contractor has to make all reasonable efforts to mitigate the delay.

The clause states that subject to sub clause 9.3 and 9.4 there shall be an extension to the Substantial Completion Date of the whole or the section equal to the amount of delay taking into account site working days only.

The Employer's Representative may act on own initiative in that he does not need to wait for notice if he considers an extension is due. This is, we presume, to protect the Employer's right to an extension of time.

All claims for extensions of time must be processed under clause 10.3. Failure to do so will defeat any entitlement.

9.3.3   The Employer's Representative may, at any time, revise a determination of an extension to the Date for Substantial Completion of the Works or any Section, but shall not bring those dates forward except by agreement with the Contractor under sub-clause 9.5 when work has been omitted.

NOTE

Under sub-clause 9.3.3 the Employer's Representative may review an assessment at any time but may not bring the Substantial Completion Date forward except with the Contractor's agreement under sub-clause 9.5 where works are omitted.

9.4   Programme Contingency

9.4.1   In this sub-clause, references to the **first threshold** and the **second threshold** are to the first threshold and the second threshold in the Schedule, part 1K.

9.4.2   The Contractor has included in the initial Contract Sum and shall include in its programme a contingency for delays to the Date for Substantial Completion of the Works caused by Compensation Events.

9.4.3   If the total number of Site Working Days' delay to Substantial Completion of the Works caused by Compensation Events (for which the Contractor would otherwise be entitled to an extension) is less than the first threshold, there shall be no extensions to the initial Date for Substantial Completion of the Works for delay caused by Compensation Events.

9.4.4   If the total number of Site Working Days' delay to Substantial Completion of the Works caused by Compensation Events (for which the Contractor would otherwise be entitled to an extension) exceeds the first threshold, there shall be deducted from the total number of Site Working Days' extension to the initial Date for Substantial Completion of the Works for delay caused by Compensation Events

(1)   the number of Site Working Days stated as the first threshold and

(2)   half the number of Site Working Days' delay to Substantial Completion of the Works caused by the Compensation Events (for which the Contractor would otherwise be entitled to an extension) after deducting the first threshold, but the total deduction under this paragraph (2) shall not exceed the second threshold.

[For example, if the first threshold is 20 Site Working Days, and the second threshold is 30 Site Working Days

- if the Contractor would otherwise be entitled to time extensions totalling 28 Site Working Days all due to Compensation Events, the time extension would be 4 Site Working Days $(28 - 20 - (8 \div 2) = 4)$.

  The deduction under paragraph (2) is $(28 - 20) \div 2 = 4$, or $8 \div 2 = 4$, which is less than the second threshold.

- if the Contractor would otherwise be entitled to time extensions totalling 90 Site Working Days all due to Compensation Events, the time extension would be 40 Site Working Days $(90 - 20 - 30 = 40)$.

  The calculation under paragraph (2) is $(90 - 20) \div 2 = 35$, but this is higher than the second threshold, so this deduction is 30, the amount of the second threshold.]

9.4.5   [This sub-clause 9.4 does not apply to extensions to the Date for Substantial Completion of a Section, nor to extensions of time resulting from Delay Events that are not Compensation Events.]

9.4.6   Use of the programme contingency provided for in this sub-clause shall be claimed and determined in accordance with this clause 9 and clause 10. In making a determination under sub-clauses 9.3 and 10.5 in respect of a delay to Substantial Completion of the Works, the Employer's Representative shall notify the Contractor and the Employer of how much of the first threshold and the second threshold have been used-up by delays to Substantial Completion of the Works caused by Compensation Events.

NOTE

This condition provides the Employer the opportunity to "buy out" a numbers of days' delay. This is referred to as the "programme contingency". The contingency for delays has to be built into the programme time and the associated costs have to be included in the tender sum. The amount of contingency days will be given to the Contractor in the Schedule, Part 1K, at tender stage. Before an extension of time is granted the days in the threshold contingency must be exceeded.

The delays must arise from Compensation Events only. The Compensation Events will be detailed by the Employer in the Schedule, Part 1, Section K.

The Contractor records and provides to the Employer's Representative details of the delays and their effect. The Employer's Representative makes the final assessment under clause 10.5.

The Employer's Representative shall notify the Contractor and the Employer of how much of the threshold is used up by the delays to the Date for Substantial Completion caused by Compensation Events.

Condition 9.4.4 refers to the first and second thresholds. This sub-clause sets out in detail the operation of the two thresholds and how they are to be dealt with.

9.5   Omissions and Reduction of Time

If a Change Order omits any of the Works, and the omission will result, or has resulted, in a reduction of the time required to complete the Works or any Section, the Date for Substantial Completion shall be reduced by any amount agreed between the Employer's Representative and the Contractor. [If there is no agreement, there shall be no reduction.]

> **NOTE**
>
> The Date for Substantial Completion can be brought forward as a result of a Change Order arising from an omission. The reduction in the Contract time to complete the Works has to be agreed with the Contractor; without agreement the Date for Substantial Completion cannot be brought forward.

9.6   Substantial Completion

9.6.1 The Contractor shall achieve Substantial Completion of the Works and each Section by its Date for Substantial Completion.

9.6.2 Within 20 working days after receiving the Contractor's request to certify Substantial Completion of the Works or a Section, the Employer's Representative shall give to the Contractor and the Employer

(1) a certificate stating the date that Substantial Completion occurred or

(2) the reasons for not issuing the certificate.

But if the Schedule, part 1H, so states, the Employer's Representative shall not be required to certify Substantial Completion of the Works or a Section before its Date for Substantial Completion. The certificate may include a list of Defects and any outstanding work [but nothing in the certificate, including the failure to list any Defect, relieves the Contractor of any obligations].

> **NOTE**
>
> The Contractor must request the Employer's Representative to issue a Certificate of Substantial Completion for the Works or a Section of the Works. The Employer's Representative has 20 working days after receiving the request to issue the certificate stating the date that Substantial Completion was achieved or to state the reasons for not issuing the certificate. Part 1H of the Schedule can state that the Employer's Representative does not have to issue the Certificate for a date earlier than the Substantial Completion Date stated in the Contract.
>
> The certificate may include a list of defects or incomplete works that the Contractor has to make good or complete.

9.7   Taking Over Part of the Works

9.7.1 The Employer may take over a part of the Works before Substantial Completion of the Works or any Section including the part, provided that the Employer's Representative first issues a notice to the Contractor at least 5 working days before the Employer intends to take over the part, the notice stating all of the following:

(1) the part to be taken over by the Employer

(2) any work remaining to be completed in that part

(3) the value, when it gets to Substantial Completion, of the part to be taken over and the proportion of the Contract Sum that this value represents

(4) the date the part will be taken over.

9.7.2 The Contractor shall have no liability for delay in completing the part to be taken over occurring after the date stated in the notice. The rate of liquidated damages for delay in achieving Substantial Completion of the Works and any relevant Section shall reduce by a fraction equal to the fraction of the Contract Sum represented by the Contract value of the part of the Works taken over, as certified by the Employer's Representative. The retention amount to be withheld under sub-clause 11.3 from interim payments until Substantial Completion shall reduce by the same fraction.

9.8　Liquidated Damages

9.8.1 If the Works do not reach Substantial Completion by the Date for Substantial Completion of the Works, the Contractor shall pay the Employer [and the Employer may deduct from payments to the Contractor] liquidated damages calculated at the rate stated in the Schedule, part 1G, for the period from the Date for Substantial Completion of the Works to the date of substantial completion of the Works.

9.8.2 If a Section does not reach Substantial Completion by its Date for Substantial Completion, the Contractor shall pay to the Employer liquidated damages calculated at the rate stated in the Schedule for the period from the Date for Substantial Completion of the Section to the date of substantial completion of the Section (or, if earlier and if the Schedule states a rate of liquidated damages for the Works, to the Date for Substantial Completion of the Works).

9.8.3 In this sub-clause 9.8 **date of substantial completion** means the date certified by the Employer's Representative that the Works or Section reached Substantial Completion.

NOTE

If the Works do not reach Substantial Completion by the stated date the Contractor shall pay the Employer, or the Employer may deduct from payments due to the Contractor, liquidated damages calculated at the rate stated in Part 1G of the Schedule. Liquidated damages may also apply to a section or sections of the Works.

In the event that the Employer's Representative does not issue the certificate of Substantial Completion as a result of incomplete works as advised in accordance with clause 9.6.2(2) then the Contractor is exposed to liquidated damages from the Employer.

GENERAL NOTES ON CLAUSE 9

Delay and Extension of Time – The Contractor shall, as soon as he becomes aware that the Works are being or are likely to be delayed, must notify the Employer's Representative of the delay and the cause. Within 40 days after becoming aware of the delay the Contractor shall provide full details of the delay and the effect on progress of the Works to the Employer's Representative.

While Condition 9.3.1 requires the Contractor to give notice of delay to the Employer's Representative, the claim for the extension of time and/or costs must be given under Condition 10.3.1, and any notice under 10.3.1 must prominently state that it is being given under Condition 10.3.

The time restraints, i.e. 40 working days after the Contractor became aware of the delay (not the notice), must be strictly adhered to.

Conditions 9.3 (Delay Events), 4.8 (Programme), 4.9 (Progress Reports) and 10.3 are closely related.

The Employer's Representative extends the Date for Substantial Completion under sub-clause 9.3.2.

In the event that a Contractor has already provided a notice and details of a delay for an event under Condition 10.3.1 the Contractor does not have to give a notice under Condition 9.3.1 for the same delay.

10 CLAIMS AND ADJUSTMENTS

10.1 Compensation Event

10.1.1 Subject to and in accordance with this sub-clause 10.1, if a Compensation Event occurs the Contract Sum shall be adjusted by the amount provided in sub-clause 10.6. However, the Contract Sum shall be increased only to the extent that all of the following apply to the Compensation Event:

(1) The Compensation Event is not a result of the Contractor's or Contractor's Personnel's act or omission or the Contractor's breach of the Contract.

(2) The Contractor cannot avoid the adverse effects of the Compensation Event and makes all reasonable efforts to minimise them.

(3) The Contractor has complied with this clause 10 in full [including giving notices and details within the time required].

(4) The Contract does not provide otherwise.

10.1.2 The Contractor's sole remedies for a Compensation Event shall be those stated in the Contract.

10.2 Quantities and Description in Bill of Quantities

If the Contractor calls for an adjustment to the Contract Sum because of a difference between the Contract value of the Works according to the quantities and descriptions in a Bill of Quantities in the Pricing Document (if any) and the Contract value of the Works according to the Works Requirements, and it is found that no increase is to be made to the Contract Sum, the Contractor shall pay the Employer the cost of having the check done.

10.3 Contractor Claims

10.3.1 If the Contractor considers that under the Contract there should be an extension of time or an adjustment to the Contract Sum, or that it has any other entitlement under or in connection with the Contract, the Contractor shall, as soon as practicable and in any event within 20 working days after it became aware, or should have become aware, of something that could result in such an entitlement, give notice of this to the Employer's Representative. The notice must be given according to sub-clause 4.14 and prominently state that it is being given under sub-clause 10.3 of the Contract. Within a further 20 working days after giving the notice, the Contractor shall give the Employer's Representative details of all of the following:

(1) all relevant facts about the claim

(2) a detailed calculation and, so far as practicable, a proposal, based on that calculation, of any adjustment to be made to the Contract Sum and of the amount of any other entitlement claimed by the Contractor

(3) if the Contractor considers that the programme contingency referred to in sub-clause 9.4 should be used or that there should be an extension of time, the information required under sub-clause 9.3, and, so far as practicable, a proposal, based on that information for any use of the programme contingency or any extension to the Date for Substantial Completion of the Works and any affected Section.

The Contractor shall give any further information about the event or circumstance requested by the Employer's Representative.

10.3.2 If the Contractor does not give notice and details in accordance with and within the time provided in this sub-clause 10.3, except where the Contractor has been required to and has given a proposal complying in full with sub-clause 10.4 [notwithstanding anything else in the Contract] the Contractor shall not be entitled to an increase to the Contract Sum or extension of time or use of the programme contingency referred to in sub-clause 9.4 [and the Employer shall be released from all liability to the Contractor in connection with the matter].

10.3.3 If the cause of the claim has a continuing effect, the Contractor shall update the information at monthly intervals

 (1) stating the extension of time and adjustment to the Contract Sum claimed for delay and cost already incurred and

 (2) so far as practicable, proposing a final adjustment to the Contract Sum and Date for Substantial Completion of the Works and any affected Section and

 (3) providing any other information the Employer's Representative reasonably requires.

10.3.4 The Contractor shall keep detailed contemporary records to substantiate any aspect of an event or circumstance about which it has given, or is entitled to give, notice under this sub-clause 10.3, and its resulting costs. These shall include any records the Employer's Representative directs the Contractor to keep. The Contractor shall give the records to the Employer's Representative if so directed.

NOTE

There are 12 Compensation Events listed in the Schedule, Part 1, Section K, with a further five (numbers 17–21) electable by the Employer. Should a Compensation Event arise, then before the Contract Sum is adjusted by the Employer's Representative the following criteria must be satisfied:

 (i) The Compensation Event is not a result of an act or omission of the Contractor or Contractor's Personnel, or the Contractor's breach of the Contract.

 (ii) The Contractor cannot avoid the adverse effects of the Compensation Event and makes all reasonable efforts to minimise them.

 (iii) The Contractor has complied with this clause 10 in full (including giving notices and details within the time required).

 (iv) The Contract does not provide otherwise.

The second criteria – that the Contractor cannot avoid the adverse effects of the Compensation Event and makes all reasonable efforts to minimise them – could be construed by the Employer's Representative as an obligation on the Contractor to accelerate or revise the programme for the Works in order to reduce or eradicate the delay.

 If the Contractor considers that there should be an extension of time or an adjustment to the Contract Sum, or if any other entitlement exists, he shall provide such notice to the Employer's Representative within 20 working days after he becomes aware, or should have been aware of something that would give rise to an entitlement. The notice must comply with Condition 4.14 (Communications) and be sent to the person identified in the Schedule, Part 1, Section A. The notice must prominently state that it is being given under sub-clause 10.3.

 Within a further 20 working days the Contractor shall provide:

 (i) All relevant facts;

 (ii) A detailed calculation and a proposal based on the calculation of the adjustment to be made to the Contract Sum and of the amount of any other entitlement claimed by the Contractor;

 (iii) Details of the amount of the contingency referred to in sub-clause 9.4 to be used, or details of the effect on programme and completion dates.

The Employer's Representative may request the Contractor to provide further information.

If the Contractor does not comply with notices, details and time scales set down in sub-clause 10.3 then the Contractor shall not be entitled to an increase in the Contract Sum or an extension of time and the Employer shall be released from all liability to the Contractor in relation to the matter.

Contractors must comply with all the requirements of the Contract as set down in Conditions 9 and 10 if they are to avail of entitlements in relation to extensions of time, Compensation Events and adjustments to the Contract. This places obligations on Contractors to maintain records and notices to a far greater degree than existed under the current GDLA and IEI Contracts. The Contractor's obligation is also set out in Condition 10.3.4.

If the cause of the claim has a continuing effect the Contractor shall update all the information at monthly intervals. The Contractor will have to:

(i)   state the extension of time and adjustment to the Contract Sum claimed in respect of any delay and cost already incurred;

(ii)   Propose a final adjustment to the Contract Sum and the Date for Substantial Completion of the Works and any affected section;

(iii)   Provide any other information that the Employer's Representative requires.

Sub-clause 10.3.4 requires the Contractor to keep contemporary records of all events under clause 10.3. The Employer's Representative may instruct the Contractor to keep such records.

10.4   Proposed Instructions

The Employer's Representative may direct the Contractor to make proposals for a proposed instruction. The Contractor shall not implement the proposed instruction unless and until the Employer's Representative has confirmed the instruction as given. Within 20 working days after the Employer's Representative directs the Contractor to make proposals, the Contractor shall give to the Employer's Representative all of the following:

(1)   a detailed calculation and proposal, based on the calculation, of any adjustment to the Contract Sum that would result from the proposed instruction

(2)   if the proposed instruction would cause a delay, the information required under sub-clause 9.3, and a proposal, based on that information for any use of the programme contingency referred to in sub-clause 9.4 or extension to the Date for Substantial Completion of the Works and any affected Section

(3)   if the proposed instruction is to omit any of the Works, a revised programme and, if appropriate, a proposed earlier Date for Substantial Completion of the Works and any affected Section

(4)   any Contractor's Documents required in connection with the proposed instruction, or a timetable for them.

NOTE

The Employer's Representative may request the Contractor to provide a proposal on a proposed instruction. The Contractor has 20 working days to provide the details, which will include:

(i)   Calculation of the adjustment to the Contract Sum;

(ii)   Details of any delay and information required under clause 9.3 with regards to the Date for Substantial Completion of the Works or any section of the Works;

(iii)   A revised programme in the case of an omission, and, if appropriate, a proposed earlier Date for Substantial Completion;

(iv)   Contractor's Documents required in relation to the proposal or a timetable for them.

The Contractor shall not implement the proposed instruction until the Employer's Representative confirms the instruction as given.

10.5   Employer's Representative's Determination

10.5.1   If the Contractor has made a claim or proposal under sub-clauses 10.3 or 10.4, the Employer's Representative shall, within 20 working days of receiving it, do one of the following:

(1)   direct the Contractor to give additional information or revised proposals, in which case the Contractor shall do so within 10 working days and the Employer's Representative shall reply in accordance with this sub-clause within a further 10 working days, but that reply must not require the Contractor to give additional information or a revised proposal

(2)   notify the Contractor and the Employer that the Contractor's proposals are agreed and make any resulting adjustments to the Contract Sum, use of the programme contingency referred to in sub-clause 9.4 or extension to the Date for Substantial Completion of the Works and any affected Section

(3)   make a determination of any adjustments to the Contract Sum, use of the programme contingency referred to in sub-clause 9.4 or extension to the Date for Substantial Completion of the Works and any affected Section, and notify the Contractor and the Employer

(4)   in response to a proposal under sub-clause 10.4, notify the Contractor that the proposed instruction will not be given.

10.5.2   The Employer's Representative may [but is not bound to] make a determination under (3) above on its own initiative if the Contractor has not made a claim or proposal under sub-clauses 10.3 or 10.4.

NOTE

The Employer's Representative has 20 working days to respond to a Contractor's claim under sub-clause 10.3 or a proposal under sub-clause 10.4. He may:

(i)   Request more information or a revised proposal – the Contractor then has 10 working to respond. The Employer's Representative then has a further 10 working days to reply;

(ii)   Notify the Employer and the Contractor that the Contractor's proposals are agreed and make any resulting adjustment to the Contract Sum, use of the programme contingency referred to in sub-clause 9.4, or extension to the date of Substantial Completion of the Works and any affected Section;

(iii)   Make a determination of the adjustment to the Contract Sum, use of the programme contingency referred to in sub-clause 9.4, or extension to the date of Substantial Completion of the Works and any affected Section, and notify the Contractor and the Employer;

(iv)   In response to a Contractor's proposal issued under sub-clause 10.4, notify the Contractor that the proposed instruction will not be given.

Where the Contractor has not made a claim under sub-clause 10.3 or submitted a proposal under sub-clause 10.4, the Employer's Representative may work (but is not bound to) on his own initiative in making an adjustment to the Contract Sum or extending the Date for Substantial Completion of the Works.

10.6   Adjustments to the Contract Sum

Adjustments to the Contract Sum for a Compensation Event shall only be for the value of any additional, substituted, and omitted work required as a result of the Compensation Event under this sub-clause 10.6 and any delay cost under sub-clause 10.7. Additional, substituted, and omitted work shall be valued as follows:

10.6.1   If the Compensation Event requires additional, substituted or omitted work, similar to work for which there are rates in the Pricing Document, to be executed under similar conditions, the determination shall use those rates.

10.6.2   If the Compensation Event requires additional, substituted or omitted work that is not similar to work for which there are rates in the Pricing Document, or is not to be executed under similar conditions, the determination shall be on the basis of the rates in the Pricing Document when that is reasonable.

10.6.3   If the adjustment cannot be determined under the above rules, the Employer's Representative shall make a fair valuation.

10.6.4   The Employer's Representative may direct that additional or substituted work required as a result of a Compensation Event be determined on the basis of the cost of performing the additional or substituted work, compared with the Contractor's cost without the Compensation Event, determined as follows:

(1)   the number of hours worked or to be worked by each category of work person stated in the Schedule, part 2E, and engaged on the work to which the Compensation Event relates, on or off the Site, multiplied in each case by the tendered daily rate for that category stated in the Schedule, part 2E and

(2)   the cost of materials used in that work, taking into account discounts and excluding VAT, plus the percentage adjustment tendered by the Contractor and stated in the Schedule, part 2E and

(3)   the cost of plant reasonably used for that work, whether hired or owned by the Contractor, at the rates in the document listed in the Schedule, part 1K (as that document may be modified according to the Schedule, part 1K) plus or minus the percentage adjustment tendered by the Contractor and included in the Schedule, part 2E. If the document listed in the Schedule does not give a rate for a plant item, a market rental rate shall be used, plus or minus the percentage adjustment.

> **NOTE**
>
> The adjustment to the Contract Sum for a Compensation Event is carried out by using rates contained in the Pricing Document, fair rates or recorded hours by the rates stated in the Schedule, Part 2E, together with the cost of plant and materials with the percentage additions quoted in the Schedule, Part 2E.
>
> The Employer's Representative may direct that additional or substituted Works required as a result of a Compensation Event be determined in accordance with the Contractor's tendered hourly labour rates and the Contractor's tendered percentage addition to the cost of plant and materials.

10.7   Delay Cost

10.7.1   If the Date for Substantial Completion of the Works has been extended because of a Compensation Event [and not otherwise, and subject to sub-clause 10.7.2], there shall be added to the Contract Sum an amount for delay cost, either (whichever it says in the Schedule, part 1K)

(1)   for each Site Working Day for which the Date for Substantial Completion of the Works has been extended because of the Compensation Event, the daily rate of delay cost tendered by the Contractor in the Schedule, part 2E or

(2)   the expenses [excluding profit and loss of profit] unavoidably incurred by the Contractor as a result of the delay to the Date for Substantial Completion of the Works caused by the Compensation Event in respect of which that date has been extended under the Contract.

10.7.2   If a delay has more than one cause, and one or more of the causes is not a Compensation Event, there shall be no increase to the Contract Sum for delay cost for the period of concurrent delay.

NOTE

Sub-clause 10.7.2 provides that if a delay has more than one cause, and one or more of the causes is not a Compensation Event, there shall be no increase to the Contract Sum for delay costs for the period of concurrent delay. This removes any dispute or ambiguity about which delay is the dominant delay and whether compensation is due to the Contractor as a result of the dominant delay.

10.7.3   If, as a result of a Compensation Event, the Date for Substantial Completion of the Works has been extended, so that there is a period of 7 or more consecutive non-working days in the time between the Starting Date and the Date for Substantial Completion of the Works, and that would not have occurred without the Compensation Event happening, then the Contractor's expenses [excluding profit and loss of profit] unavoidably incurred because of this delay shall be included in the determination of the addition to the Contract Sum for delay cost. But the amount so added shall not exceed the amount stated in the Schedule, part 2E, as the Contractor's tendered rate of delay cost multiplied by the number of additional non-working days, if there is an amount stated there. **Non-working day** means a day that, for good reason, is not a Site Working Day [such as a trade holiday].

10.7.4   Except as provided in this sub-clause 10.7 [notwithstanding anything else in the Contract] losses or expenses arising from or in connection with delay, disruption, loss of productivity or knock-on effect shall not be taken into account or included in any increase to the Contract Sum, and the Employer shall have no liability for such losses or expenses.

10.7.5   [There shall be no delay cost paid as a result of extensions to the Date for Substantial Completion of a Section].

10.7.6   If the Schedule states more than one rate for delay cost, the rate for the period when the delay occurred or delayed part of the Works shall be used. This shall be determined by the Employer's Representative.

NOTE

Delay costs are added as defined in the Schedule, Part 2 E. The Contractor's delay costs are capped to that stated in the Schedule. Sub-clause 10.7.2 provides for holiday(s) within an extended period to payment for costs incurred, but the costs are capped at the daily delay cost tendered rate stated in the Schedule, Part 2E.

Losses or expenses arising from or in relation to delay, disruption, loss of productivity or knock-on effect shall not be taken into account or included in any assessment of an increase to the Contract Sum. The Employer has no liability for such losses or expenses.

There will be no delay costs paid as a result of extensions to the Date for Substantial Completion of a Section.

10.8   Price Variation

The Contract includes clause PV1 or clause PV2, whichever is stated in the Schedule, Part 1M.

NOTE

Sub-clause 10.8 deals with price variation. There are two approaches electable at the discretion of the Employer in the Schedule, Part 1:

   (i)   The Proven Cost Method (PV1);

         This is an invoice-based system whereby the Contractor establishes his entitlement after the fixed-price period by invoices which are checked by the Employer. The definiition of Base Date under PV1 is the first day of the thirty-first month after the Contract date, so that this approach guarantees the Employer the 30-month fixed price even if there should be a delay in setting the Contract Date.

> (ii)   The Formula Fluctuations Method (PV2).
>
>> This is based on the use of CSO Indices for different categories of materials, fuels and CPI, as published in the Wholesale Price Indices. The weighting for each of the materials, fuel, labour, non-reusable temporary works and non-recoverable overheads are established by the Employer and the proportions of different fuels and materials are also defined for use with these indices, and these proportions are provided in the Invitation to Tender.

10.9   Employer's Claims

10.9.1   If the Employer or the Employer's Representative considers that, under the Contract, there should be an adjustment to the Contract Sum, or that any amount is due to the Employer from the Contractor under the Contract, the Employer or the Employer's Representative shall, as soon as practicable, give notice and particulars of the event or circumstances to the other, and to the Contractor. The notice shall include

  (1)   details of the event or circumstances giving rise to the notice, and all relevant facts and

  (2)   a calculation, and a proposal based on that calculation, of any adjustment to be made to the Contract Sum or any amount due by the Contractor to the Employer.

10.9.2   The Contractor shall be entitled, within 20 working days of receipt of such a notice, to give a response to the Employer's Representative and shall, if the notice was given by the Employer, give a copy of any response to the Employer. Within 20 working days after receiving the Contractor's response, or after the time for responding has elapsed, if the Contractor has not responded within that time, the Employer's Representative shall determine the matter in accordance with the Contract.

10.9.3   The Employer may deduct from any amount due to the Contractor

  (1)   any amount determined by the Employer's Representative to be due, or likely to become due, from the Contractor to the Employer under the Contract and

  (2)   any amount due from the Contractor to the Employer under any contract.

10.9.4   The procedure in this sub-clause 10.9 shall apply until either the Defects Certificate or the certificates required following termination have been issued, but this does not limit the Employer's rights after then.

NOTE

The Contractor can be liable to the Employer for any monies the Employer or the Employer's Representative may consider due to the Employer. The Contractor shall pay these monies to the Employer or the Employer may deduct the money from payments on the particular project or any other contract.

The Employer's claims are not time-barred as the Contractor's are under sub-clause 10.3. The Contractor has 20 working days to respond to such a notice to the Employer's Representative and the Employer (if the notice was sent by the Employer). The Employer Representative has 20 working days to consider the matter.

Notice of the event and a calculation of the adjustment to the Contract Sum must be provided to the Contractor by either the Employer or the Employer's Representative before any adjustments can be made to the Contract Sum.

GENERAL NOTES ON CLAUSE 10

This clause deals with the manner in which both Delay Events and compensation costs will be evaluated. This is an innovative approach to the management of claims, requiring strict adherence to procedures in order to preserve an entitlement to claim.

Every single event in respect of which compensation is to be claimed must be processed under sub-clause 10.3. The amount of detail required is substantial and where the claim arises, for example, from an instructed variation, the requirement and responsibility to furnish the notice and the documentation rests with the Contractor. Notices, within the specified time periods, must be submitted in order to preserve entitlements.

Schedule 1, Section K, is central to the Contract, as the lists contained in the Schedule set out when compensation will be payable and when extensions of time can be granted.

Sub-clause 10.4 provides that, prior to issuing an instruction, the Employer's Representative can instruct the Contractor to prepare an assessment, in terms of time and money, of a proposed instruction. The Contractor should note the additional burden placed upon him in the preparation of documents and programmes for a Work Item that may not proceed. There is no provision for the Employer to compensate the Contractor for any administration work or associated costs.

In practical terms this is a Fixed Price Lump Sum Contract which does not allow for price variation in any meaningful way except for increases in PRSI, VAT and excise duties which can be reimbursed at cost.

11   PAYMENT

11.1   Interim Payment

11.1.1   At each of the following times

(i)   the periods for interim payment stated in the Schedule, part 1L, if the amount payable is more than the minimum amount stated in the Schedule and

(ii)   upon issue of the certificate of Substantial Completion for the Works or any Section

the Contractor shall give a statement to the Employer's Representative showing all of the following:

(1)   the progress of the Works

(2)   the instalment of the Contract Sum that the Contractor considers should, under the Contract, be paid on an interim basis

(3)   a detailed breakdown

(4)   any supporting evidence the Employer's Representative requires.

The statement given on Substantial Completion shall include all amounts due to the Contractor for the Works or Section.

11.1.2   The instalment of the Contract Sum that the Contractor shall be entitled to be paid on an interim basis shall be

(1)   the Contract value of the Works properly executed by the Contractor [according to the Pricing Document] and

(2)   any amount the Employer's Representative considers proper under sub-clause 11.2 and

(3)   amounts for adjustments to the Contract Sum for Compensation Events, as determined under the Contract and

(4)   any amount to be paid according to clause PV1 or PV2, whichever is part of the Contract.

11.1.3   Within 10 working days of receipt of the Contractor's statement the Employer's Representative shall give the Contractor a certificate, sending a copy to the Employer, setting out the amount of interim payment that, in the Employer's Representative's opinion, is to be made by the Employer to the Contractor, taking account of any amount due from the Contractor to the Employer [including damages for delay], together with calculations and the reasons for the opinion.

11.1.4   If there is a sum due to the Contractor, the Contractor shall send an invoice to the Employer for that sum after receiving the interim certificate. The Employer shall pay the amount due on the invoice within 15 working days after receiving the invoice.

NOTE

The time of Interim Payments will be stated in Part 1L of the Schedule. At the time for an Interim Payment the Contractor shall provide to the Employer's Representative a statement showing:

(i)   the progress of the Works;

(ii)   the instalment that the Contractor should be paid;

(iii)   a detailed breakdown;

(iv) any supporting details the Employer's Representative requires;

(v) Not stated in sub-clause 11.1.2 but contained in sub-clause 5.3.7, the Contractor must supply with each Interim Statement a Certificate stating that the Contractor has complied in full with sub-clause 5.3 (Pay and Conditions of Employment); see sub-clause 11.4.4 for the severe effect of non-compliance with sub-clause 5.3.7.

Within 10 days of receipt of the Contractor's Interim Statement the Employer's Representative shall issue a Certificate setting out the amounts due to the Contractor (if any) after taking account of any amount due from the Contractor to the Employer including damages for delay. The Employer's Representative has to provide the calculations and reasons for his opinion in support of the Certificate.

The Contractor has to provide an invoice to the Employer for any amount due to him as directed by the Payment Certificate. The Employer then pays the amount within 15 days after receipt of the invoice.

Interim Payment Statement	Certificate	Invoice	Payment
1st of month	10th of month	11th of month	26th of month

Note: Allowance has to be made for weekends, public holidays, annual industry holidays and any other non-working day specified in the Contract.

11.2   Unfixed Works Items

At the discretion of the Employer's Representative, but only when so provided in the Pricing Document, interim payments may include any amount, not exceeding the percentage of value stated in the Schedule, part 1L, the Employer's Representative considers proper for each of the following:

(1) the Contract value of any Works Items that comply with all of the following requirements, all to the satisfaction of the Employer's Representative:

   (a) they have been completed and are substantially ready to be incorporated in the Works

   (b) title to them has been vested in the Employer

   (c) they are stored suitably at the Site

   (d) they have not been delivered to the Site prematurely

(2) the Contract value of any Work Items not delivered to the Site that comply with all of the following requirements, all to the satisfaction of the Employer's Representative:

   (a) they have been completed and are substantially ready to be incorporated in the Works

   (b) title to them has been vested in the Employer

   (c) they are stored suitably and set aside and marked to show clearly that their destination is the Site and that they are the property of the Employer

   (d) they are clearly identified in a list given to the Employer's Representative, together with documentary evidence that title is vested in the Employer

   (e) they are insured as required by the Contract, and will be insured as required while in transit

   (f) the Contractor has given the Employer a bond in the form for such bonds in the Works Requirements, or if there is none, a form approved by the Employer, executed by a surety approved by the Employer's Representative, for the amount to be paid.

NOTE

The Contractor can be paid for unfixed Works Items up to a value of 90 percent provided that the Contract allows a provision for a higher value which will be detailed in Part 1L of the Schedule, provided that:

(i)   they have been completed and they are substantially ready to be incorporated into the Works;

(ii) title to them has been vested in the Employer;

(iii) they are stored suitably on site;

(iv) they have not been brought to the site prematurely.

Payment for unfixed Work Items is at the discretion of the Employer's Representative.

Payment for goods not delivered to the site is governed by the following:

(i)   they have been completed and are substantially ready to be incorporated in the Works;

(ii) title to them has been vested in the Employer;

(iii) they are stored suitably and marked to show that they are the property of the Employer and that their destination is the site;

(iv) They are clearly identified in a list provided to the Employer's Representative and with documentary evidence that title is vested in the Employer;

(v)   They are insured as required by the Contract and will be insured while in transit;

(vi) The Employer is provided with a bond by a surety approved by the Employer's Representative for the amount to be paid.

11.3   Retention

11.3.1   The Employer may deduct from any interim payment to the Contractor the retention percentage stated in the Schedule, part 1L.

11.3.2   Upon issue of the certificate of Substantial Completion of the Works, the Contractor shall be entitled to invoice the Employer for half of the amount so retained. Upon the issue of the Defects Certificate, the Contractor shall be entitled to invoice the Employer for the balance of the money so retained.

11.3.3   If, within 10 working days of the issue of the certificate of Substantial Completion of the Works, or another date agreed by the Employer's Representative, the Contractor provides to the Employer a retention bond in the form in the Work Requirements, or, if there is none, a form approved by the Employer, for the amount retained by the Employer, and executed by a surety approved by the Employer, the Contractor shall be entitled to invoice the Employer for the balance of the money retained.

11.3.4   Upon issue of the certificate of Substantial Completion of a Section of the Works, the retention amount to be withheld until issue of the certificate of Substantial Completion of the Works shall be reduced by the amount stated in the Schedule, part 1G, and the Contractor shall be entitled to invoice the Employer for that amount.

11.3.5   The Employer shall pay the Contractor the amount due on an invoice under this sub-clause 11.3 within 15 working days after receiving the invoice [less any amount that the Employer is entitled to deduct according to sub-clause 10.9].

11.4   Full Payment

The payments to the Contractor under this Contract are for compliance in full with the Contractor's obligations to the time of payment [including construction management, programming, reporting, payment of wages and observing employment requirements] [but payment does not imply acceptance that the obligations have been performed]. When the Contractor has not fully complied with its obligations, the Employer is not required to make payment in full [without limiting its other rights or remedies]. In particular

11.4.1 If the Contractor has not given a collateral warranty by the date stated in the Schedule, part 1F, the Employer is entitled to deduct from payment to the Contractor the amount stated in the Schedule, part 1F until the collateral warranty is given.

11.4.2 If the Contractor has not submitted a programme or given a progress report when required by sub-clauses 4.9 and 4.10, the Employer may deduct 15% of each payment to the Contractor until the programme or report has been submitted or given.

11.4.3 If the Contractor has not complied with sub-clause 5.3, the Employer shall be entitled to make the deduction provided for in sub-clause 5.3.6.

11.4.4 If the Contractor does not give the certificate required by sub-clause 5.3.7 with an interim statement, there shall be no payment due under sub-clause 11.1 for the relevant Work Item until the certificate is given.

11.4.5 Deductions from payments because of obligations that the Contractor has still not complied with by the date the Defects Certificate was issued shall be deducted from the Contract Sum. In the case of a deduction from the Contract Sum because of failure to give the certificate required by sub-clause 5.3.7, the amount deducted shall be the portion of the Contract value of the relevant Work Item that the Employer determines to be the labour portion. The Contractor shall give the Employer any information the Employer requires for this determination.

NOTE

Full payment is dependent on:

    (i)   The Contractor has providing all the collateral warranties, otherwise the Employer may deduct the amount stated in Part1F of the Schedule.

   (ii)   The Contractor submitting a programme or a revised programme or progress report otherwise the Employer may deduct 15% of each payment until the programme and/or reports are submitted.

  (iii)   The Contractor complying with sub-clause 5.3 (Pay and Conditions of Employment), otherwise the Employer may make the deduction provided for in sub-clause 5.3.6.

  (iv)   The Contractor providing a Certificate as required by sub-clause 5.3.7, otherwise there shall be no payment due for the relevant Work Item until the Certificate is submitted or provided.

   (v)   The Contractor complying with all his obligations by the date the Defects Certificate is issued.

If there is any deduction to the Contract Sum as a result of the Contractor's failure to provide the Certificate required by sub-clause 5.3.7, the amount deducted shall be the labour-element value for the portion of Works, as determined by the Employer. The Contractor has to provide the Employer with any information the Employer requires in order to make the determination.

11.5   Final Statement

11.5.1 Within 2 months after Substantial Completion of the Works is certified, the Contractor shall give to the Employer's Representative a final statement. The Contractor shall include in that statement all money that the Contractor considers to be due from the Employer to the Contractor under or in connection with the Contract. The Employer shall have no liability to the Contractor under or in connection with the Contract for any matter not detailed in the final statement, except under the indemnities in the Contract or Compensation Events occurring after Substantial Completion of the Works was certified.

11.5.2 Within 3 months after receipt of the Contractor's final statement, or if no final statement is issued within the time required, within 5 months after Substantial Completion of the Works is certified, the Employer's Representative shall issue to the Contractor and to the Employer a penultimate payment certificate certifying the amount that, in the Employer's Representative's opinion, will be due from the Employer to the Contractor, less any final retention to be paid after the Defects Certificate is issued, or from the Contractor to the Employer.

11.5.3 As soon as practicable, no more than 3 months, after the Defects Certificate is issued, the Employer's Representative shall issue a final payment certificate certifying the amount that, in the Employer's Representative's opinion, is finally due from the Employer to the Contractor, or from the Contractor to the Employer. The amount in the final payment certificate shall be the same as the amount in the penultimate payment certificate, except for

(1) the final payment of retention and

(2) adjustments to the Contract Sum because of Compensation Events that happen after Substantial Completion of the Works is certified and

(3) amounts owed by the Contractor that were not included in the penultimate certificate [for example, for Defects that the Contractor has not rectified] and

(4) deductions from the Contract Sum under sub-clause 11.4.

11.5.4 If the penultimate or final payment certificate states that there is a sum owing to the Contractor, the Contractor shall issue an invoice to the Employer for that sum and the Employer shall pay the amount due on the invoice within 15 working days after receiving the invoice. If the penultimate or final payment certificate states that there is a sum owing to the Employer, the Contractor shall pay the amount due within 10 working days of receipt of the Employer's demand for payment. [Payments and certificates, including the penultimate and final payment certificates and the Defects Certificate, will not relieve the Contractor of any obligations, or be evidence of the value of work or that work has been completed satisfactorily].

NOTE

Within two months after Substantial Completion is certified, the Contractor shall provide a Final Statement which shall include all money that the Contractor considers due from the Employer. The Employer shall have no liability to the Contractor for any matter not detailed in the Final Statement except for indemnities or Compensation Events occurring after Substantial Completion was certified. This means the Contractor will have to compile the Final Account as the Works are ongoing. The Contractor must ensure that subcontractors also provide details of their accounts diligently to the Contractor for incorporation into the Final Statement.

The Contractor's Final Statement must be a comprehensive document that includes all items that the Contractor claims payment for.

Contract Completion	Contractor's Final Statement	Employer's Representative's Penultimate Certificate
1	2 months	3 months or 5 months after Substantial Completion is certified

5 months total, or 7 months in the event that the Contractor does not provide a Final Statement

The Final Certificate cannot adjust any value(s) contained in the Penultimate Certificate. Similarly items for which the Contractor claims payment that were not included in his Final Statement cannot be included in the Final Certificate. The onus is on the Contractor to ensure that his Final Statement is a comprehensive document.

> Monies to be paid to the Contractor as detailed in the Penultimate or Final Certificate shall become due and be paid by the Employer within 15 working days after receipt by the Employer of the Contractor's invoice.
>
> Monies to be paid by the Contractor to the Employer as detailed in the Penultimate or Final Certificate shall be paid by the Contractor within 10 working days of receipt of the Employer's demand.
>
> Payments and Certificates (Interim Payment Certificates, Penultimate Certificates, Final Certificate and Defects Certificates) will not be evidence that the Works have been carried out satisfactorily or relieve the Contractor of any of his contractual obligations.
>
> Late payments attract interest at the rate provided in the European Communities (Late Payment in Commercial Transactions) Regulations 2002.

11.6   Time for Payment and Interest

11.6.1 When a payment is to be made under the Contract, and no time for payment is stated, the amount due shall be paid within 30 days of receipt of a demand for payment.

11.6.2 Interest shall be added to any payment not made within the time provided in the Contract, from the date the payment was due under the Contract, at the rate provided in the European Communities (Late Payment in Commercial Transactions) Regulations 2002.

11.7   Value Added Tax

11.7.1 The Contract Sum includes value-added tax (**VAT**). All other amounts in the Contract, unless otherwise stated, exclude VAT.

11.7.2 Adjustments to the Contract Sum shall be on a net-of-VAT basis, and the appropriate sum for VAT shall be added or subtracted.

11.7.3 The Contractor shall send the Employer, for each payment, an invoice complying with section 17 of the Value-Added Tax Act 1972.

11.8   Withholding Tax

The Employer shall be entitled to make any deduction or withholding on account of tax required by Legal Requirements or the practice of the Revenue Commissioners.

12 TERMINATION

12.1 Termination on Contractor Default

12.1.1 The Employer may, without limiting any other right or remedy, terminate the Contractor's obligation to complete the Works by notice to the Contractor if any of the following occurs:

(1) the Contractor fails to comply with its obligations under the Contract, and, if the failure can be cured, the Employer's Representative has directed the Contractor to put the matter right, and the Contractor has not done so within 14 days after receiving the direction

(2) the Contractor abandons or, except where required or permitted by the Contract, suspends the execution of the Works

(3) the Contractor fails to proceed regularly and diligently with the execution of the Works

(4) the Contractor fails to maintain the required insurances or performance bond

(5) the Starting Date has not occurred or the Contractor has not started to execute the Works on the Site within 6 weeks of the date the Contract requires

(6) any of the Contractor's warranties in sub-clause 2.5.2 or sub-clause 2.6 are untrue

(7) the Contractor has committed or caused the Employer to commit a serious breach of Legal Requirements concerning the Works

(8) the Contractor or Contractor's Personnel have committed a breach of the Safety, Health and Welfare at Work Act 2005 or any regulations or code of practice made under it concerning the Works

(9) the Contractor has not complied with sub-clauses 5.3.2 or 5.3.3 either (a) within 14 days after notice from the Employer requiring a failure to be put right or (b) persistently

(10) the Contractor has subcontracted all or any part of the Works in breach of the Contract

(11) any of the following **insolvency events** occur:

(a) a petition for the appointment of a liquidator to the Contractor is presented and is not dismissed within 10 working days of presentation

(b) any meeting of creditors of the Contractor is convened or held

(c) any arrangement or composition with or for the benefit of its creditors [including any compromises or arrangements entered into under sections 201 to 204 of the Companies Act 1963] are proposed or entered into by or in respect of the Contractor

(d) a supervisor, receiver, administrator, administrative receiver, trustee or encumbrancer takes possession of or is appointed over the Contractor, or any distress, execution or other process is levied or enforced, and not discharged within 10 working days, on the Contractor or any of its assets

(e) the Contractor ceases or threatens to cease carrying on business, or is, or is regarded by law or by a court to be, or declares itself to be, insolvent or unable to pay its debts as they fall due

(f) a petition is presented to appoint an examiner to the Contractor, or an order is made appointing an examiner to the Contractor

(g) the Contractor, being an individual, becomes bankrupt

(h) any event similar to the above insolvency events occurs in respect of the Contractor in any jurisdiction in which it is incorporated or has a place of business

(12) the Contractor, if an individual, dies or becomes incapable of performing the Contract.

12.1.2 If the Contractor is more than one person, if any of the insolvency events occur in respect of any of them, the Employer may either

(1) terminate the Contractor's obligation to complete the Works or

(2) terminate the obligation to complete the Works of the person concerned and the others shall remain liable to perform the Contractor's obligations.

12.1.3 If any insolvency events occur in respect of any person who has guaranteed the Contractor's performance of the Contract to the Employer, or a guarantee ceases to be enforceable against the guarantor, the Employer may terminate the Contractor's obligation to complete the Works unless, within 10 working days of the event, the Contractor has arranged a replacement guarantee and guarantor to the Employer's satisfaction.

NOTE

Grounds for termination by the Employer are:

(i)   The Contractor fails to comply with his obligations under the Contract;

(ii)   The Contractor suspends or abandons the Works;

(iii)   The Contractor fails to proceed regularly and diligently;

(iv)   The Contractor fails to provide the required insurances or performance bond;

(v)   The starting has not occurred or the Contractor has not commenced the Works on site within six weeks of the Contract Date;

(vi)   Any of the Contractor's warranties in sub-clause 2.5.2 (Safety, Health and Welfare) or sub-clause 2.6 (Ethics in Public Office) are untrue;

(vii)   The Contractor committed or caused the Employer to commit a serious breach of Legal Requirements in relation to the Works;

(viii)   The Contractor committed a breach of the Safety Health and Welfare at Work Act 2005;

(ix)   The Contractor has not complied with sub-clause 5.3.2 or 5.3.3 (Pay and Conditions of Employment);

(x)   The Contractor has subcontracted all or part of the Works in breach of the Contract;

(xi)   Insolvency (eight issues);

(xii)   The Contractor, if an individual, dies or becomes incapable of performing the Contract.

12.2   Consequences of Default Termination

If the Contractor's obligation to complete the Works is terminated under sub-clause 12.1, the following shall apply:

12.2.1 The Contractor shall leave the Site in an orderly manner.

12.2.2 Payment of all sums of money that may then be due from the Employer to the Contractor shall be postponed, and the Employer shall not be required to make any further payment to the Contractor except as provided in this sub-clause.

12.2.3 The Employer's Representative shall, as soon as practicable, determine the amount due to the Contractor under the Contract for the Works completed in accordance with the Contract and unpaid (the **termination value**).

12.2.4 The Contractor shall not remove any Works Items or Contractor's Things from the Site unless directed to do so by the Employer, and if directed, shall promptly remove from the Site any Works Items and Contractor's Things, as directed.

12.2.5 The Employer may engage other contractors, use any Works Items and Contractor's Things on the Site and do anything necessary for the completion of the Works.

12.2.6 The Contractor shall, if so directed by the Employer's Representative, assign to the Employer [without further payment] the benefit of any subcontract, contract for the supply of any Works Item, or other contract concerning the Contract.

12.2.7 The Employer may pay to any Subcontractor or supplier to the Contractor any amount due to it that the Employer's Representative certifies as included in any previous interim payment to the Contractor. The Contractor shall re-pay to the Employer such an amount on request.

12.2.8 The Contractor shall give the Employer all Works Requirements and Contractor's Documents it [or Contractor's Personnel] has.

12.2.9 When the Works have been completed and the termination amount as described below has been determined, the Employer's Representative shall give a certificate to the Contractor and the Employer setting out the total of the following (the **termination amount**):

(1) the Employer's additional cost of completing the Works compared with the cost that would have been incurred if the Works had been completed by the Contractor in accordance with the Contract

(2) loss and damage incurred by the Employer as a result of the termination and its cause

(3) amounts due to the Employer by the Contractor under or in connection with the Contract or in connection with the Works.

12.2.10 If the Employer does not begin to put in place arrangements to complete the Works within 6 months after the termination, the Employer's Representative shall issue this certificate as soon as practicable after the end of this 6 month period, based, if necessary, on estimates.

12.2.11 If the termination amount is less than the termination value, the Contractor shall issue an invoice to the Employer for the difference and the Employer shall pay the amount due on the invoice within 15 working days after receiving the invoice. If the termination amount is more than the termination value, the Contractor shall pay the Employer the difference within 10 working days of receiving the Employer's demand for payment.

NOTE

The consequences of default termination are:

(i) The Contractor is obliged to leave the site in an orderly manner.

(ii) Payment of any monies due to the Contractor are postponed and the Employer shall not be required to make any further payment to the Contractor except as provided in clause 12.2.

(iii) The Employer's Representative, as soon as is practicable, make an assessment of the amount due to the Contractor in respect of Works completed in accordance with the Contract and unpaid. This is the *Termination Value*.

(iv) The Contractor cannot remove any Works Items or things from the site unless instructed to do so by the Employer.

(v) The Employer may engage other Contractors, use any Works Items and Contractor's Things on the site and do any thing necessary for the completion of the Works.

(vi) If instructed by the Employer's Representative, the Contractor shall assign to the Employer, without further payment, the benefit of any subcontract, contract for supply, or other contract in relation to the performance of the Works.

(vii)   The Employer may pay to any subcontractor or supplier to the Contractor any amount due to it that the Employer's Representative certifies as included in any previous interim payment. The Contractor shall repay to the Employer such an amount on request.

(viii) The Contractor provides to the Employer all Work Requirements and Contractor's Documents.

(ix)   When the Works have been completed and the *Termination Amount* has been assessed, the Employer's Representative shall certify the Termination Amount setting out:

    (a)   the Employer's additional cost of completing the Works compared with the cost that would have been incurred if the Works had been completed by the Contractor;

    (b)   Loss and damage incurred by the Employer as a result of the termination and its cause;

    (c)   Amounts due to the Employer by the Contractor.

(x)   If the Employer does not begin to put in place arrangements for the completion of the Works within six months of the termination, the Employer's Representative shall issue the certificate as soon as possible, after the end of the six-month period based, where necessary, on estimates. If the *Termination Amount* is less than the *Termination Value* the Contractor shall raise an invoice for the difference and the Employer shall pay that amount within 15 days of receipt of the invoice. If the *Termination Amount* is more than the *Termination Value* the Contractor shall pay to the Employer the difference within 10 working days of receiving the Employer's demand for payment.

12.3   Suspension by the Contractor

If the Employer fails to pay any amount due under a certificate issued by the Employer's Representative under the Contract, the Contractor may make of the Employer a written demand for payment, and if the payment has not been made within 15 working days of the receipt of the demand, the Contractor may, on giving notice to the Employer, suspend execution of the Works until the amount has been paid. On receiving the payment, the Contractor shall resume execution of the Works.

> **NOTE**
>
> If the Employer fails to make payment under a payment certificate the Contractor shall make a written demand for payment to the Employer. If the payment is not made within a further 15 working days of the receipt of the demand, the Contractor may, on written notice to the Employer, suspend the Works until payment is received. Upon receipt of payment the Contractor shall resume execution of the Works.

12.4   Termination by the Contractor

The Contractor shall be entitled to terminate the Contractor's obligation to complete the Works by notice to the Employer if any of the following occur:

(1)   the Contractor has suspended the execution of the Works for 15 working days in accordance with sub-clause 12.3, and the Employer has still not paid

(2)   work has been suspended by direction of the Employer's Representative under sub-clause 9.2 and a right to terminate has arisen under that sub-clause

(3)   the execution of the Works or a substantial part of the Works has been suspended for a period of at least 3 months as a consequence of loss or damage that is at the Employer's risk under sub-clause 3.1

(4)   an event or circumstance outside the control of the parties makes it physically impossible or contrary to Law for the Contractor to fulfil its obligations under the Contract for a period of at least 6 months.

NOTE

The Contractor may terminate by notice to the Employer if:

    (i)   The Contractor has suspended the Works for 15 working days in accordance with sub-clause 12.3 (Suspension by the Contractor) and the payment has not been made.

    (ii) Work has been suspended under an instruction by the Employer's Representative under sub-clause 9.2 (Suspension) and a right to terminate has arisen under that sub-clause.

    (iii) Work or a substantial part of it has been suspended for a period at least three months as a consequence of loss or damage that is at the Employer's risk.

    (iv) An event occurs that is outside the control of the parties and that makes it physically impossible or contrary to law for the Contractor to fulfil his obligations for a period of at least 6 months.

12.5 Termination at Employer's Election

12.5.1 The Employer shall be entitled to terminate the Contractor's obligation to complete the Works at its election on 20 working days notice to the Contractor.

12.5.2 The Employer may not terminate the Contractor's obligation to complete the Works under this sub-clause 12.5 for the purpose of retaining another contractor to execute the Works.

12.5.3 The Employer shall return any performance bond required under this Contract to the Contractor on termination under this sub-clause 12.5.

NOTE

The Employer is entitled to terminate the Contract upon 20 days' notice to the Contractor. The Employer cannot engage another Contractor to complete the Works. The Employer must return the performance bond to the Contractor.

12.6 Consequences of Termination by Contractor or at Employer's Election

If the Contractor's obligation to complete the Works is terminated under sub-clause 12.4 or sub-clause 12.5 the following shall apply:

12.6.1 The Contractor shall leave the Site in an orderly manner and remove any Contractor's Things.

12.6.2 The Contractor shall give the Employer all Works Requirements and all Contractor's Documents.

12.6.3 The Contractor shall, as soon as practicable, give the Employer's Representative a statement of the total of the following (the **termination sum**):

    (1) the unpaid value of the parts of the Works completed to the date of termination in accordance with the Pricing Document, disregarding any provision limiting the Employer's obligation to pay for partially completed work

    (2) the Contractor's reasonable costs of removal from the Site as a consequence of the termination

    (3) all other amounts due to the Contractor under the Contract but not damages.

12.6.4 Within 10 working days of receiving this statement, the Employer's Representative shall issue a certificate to the Contractor and the Employer of the amount due from the Contractor to the Employer or the Employer to the Contractor, including the termination sum in the calculation of the amount due from the Employer to the Contractor. If the certificate shows an amount owing to the Contractor, the Contractor shall issue an invoice to the Employer for that amount, and the Employer shall pay the amount due on the invoice within 15 working days after receiving the invoice. If the certificate shows an amount due to the Employer, the Contractor shall pay the amount due within 10 working days of receiving the Employer's demand for payment.

> **NOTE**
>
> The following shall apply as a consequence of Termination by Contractor or at Employer's Election:
>
> (i)　The Contractor shall as soon as practicable provide the Employer's Representative with a statement of the following (the Termination Sum):
>
> > (a)　the unpaid value of the Works completed to the date of the termination
> >
> > (b)　the Contractor's reasonable costs of removal from site as a result of the termination
> >
> > (c)　all other amounts to which the Contractor is entitled under the Contract.
>
> (ii)　Within 10 working of receipt of the statement the Employer's Representative shall issue a certificate indicating the amount due from the Contractor to the Employer or the amount from the Employer to the Contractor. The Contractor shall issue an invoice to the Employer and the Employer shall pay the Contractor within 15 working days of receipt of the invoice. In the event of an amount due to the Employer the Contractor shall pay that amount within 10 working days of receiving the Employer's demand.
>
> (iii)　After termination of the Contract the Contractor's obligations survive.
>
> (iv)　The Employer's liability to the Contractor is limited to the amount payable under clause 12 and any other amount that fell due under the Contract before the termination.

12.7　Survival

Termination of the Contractor's obligation to complete the Works shall not affect the Contractor's obligations under the Contract, other than the obligation to complete the Works. [In particular the following provisions of the Contract continue to have effect after termination: sub-clauses 1.1, 1.2, 1.3, 1.4, 1.7, 1.8, 1.9, 2.1, 2.6, 3.4, 3.5, 4.16, 4.17, clause 6, this clause 12 and clause 13.]

12.8　Payment

On termination of the Contractor's obligation to complete the Works, the Employer's liability to the Contractor under or in connection with the Contract shall be limited to payment of the amount provided for in this clause 12, and any other amount that fell due under the Contract before the termination.

12.9　Reference to Conciliation

12.9.1　The Employer may [but is not required to] refer to conciliation under sub-clause 13.1 the issue of whether the Employer has become entitled to terminate the Contractor's obligation to complete the Works under sub-clause 12.1.

12.9.2　Sub-clause 13.1 shall apply to the conciliation, except that the conciliator's time to give the recommendation shall be 21 days after appointment. Clause 13.5 shall also apply.

12.9.3　If the conciliator recommends that the Employer is entitled to terminate the Contractor's obligation to complete the Works under sub-clause 12.1, and the Employer does so within 60 days after receiving the conciliator's recommendation, and it is subsequently found that the Employer was not entitled to do so, then the following shall apply:

(1)　the termination shall stand [even if the circumstances have changed] and have effect as if the Employer's termination notice under sub-clause 12.1 was a valid termination notice under sub-clause 12.5.1

(2)   sub-clauses 12.6.1 to 12.6.4 inclusive shall apply retrospectively from the date of the termination notice under sub-clause 12.1

(3)   sub-clause 12.5.2 shall not apply

(4)   the Contractor shall have no other rights or remedies under the Contract or otherwise at law for the termination.

NOTE

The Employer may refer to conciliation the issue of whether the Employer has become entitled to terminate the Contractor's obligations. The conciliator's time to give his recommendation is 21 days after his appointment. If it was subsequently found that the Employer was not entitled to terminate the Contractor's obligations then:

(i)   the termination shall stand;

(ii)   sub-clauses 12.6.1 to 12.6.4 (Consequences of Termination by Contractor or at Employer's Election) shall apply retrospectively from the date of the termination notice;

(iii) Sub-clause 12.5.2 shall not apply;

(iv)   The Contractor shall have no other rights or remedies under the Contract or otherwise at law.

If the conciliator agrees that a termination breach has occurred, the Employer decides whether or not he will act on that determination. If the Employer decides to terminate and an Arbitrator subsequently finds that the decision to terminate was incorrect, the rights of the Contractor are restricted to the rights the Contractor would have had if the Contract had been terminated at the election of the Employer – value of works to the date of termination and reasonable demobilisation costs.

13 DISPUTES

13.1 Conciliation

13.1.1   If a dispute arises under the Contract, either party may, by notice to the other, refer the dispute for conciliation under this sub-clause 13.1. The notice shall state that it is given under sub-clause 13.1 of the Contract.

13.1.2   Within 10 working days of the referral of a dispute to conciliation, the parties shall jointly appoint a conciliator who is competent to adjudicate upon the dispute and independent of the parties. If the parties fail to appoint a conciliator within 10 working days of the referral, or if a person appointed refuses to act or becomes unable to act, the conciliator shall be appointed by the appointing body or person named in the Schedule, part 1N, on the application of either party. If there is a fee for making the appointment, the parties shall share it equally. If one party pays the entire fee, it shall be entitled to reimbursement of the other party's share from the other party on demand.

13.1.3   Each party shall, within the period set by the conciliator, send to the conciliator and the other party brief details of the dispute stating its contentions as to the facts and the parties' rights and obligations concerning the dispute. The conciliator may, for this purpose, suggest further actions or investigations that may be of assistance.

13.1.4   The parties shall promptly make available to the conciliator all information, documents, access to the Site and appropriate facilities that the conciliator requires to resolve the dispute.

13.1.5   The conciliator shall consult with the parties in an attempt to resolve the dispute by agreement. The conciliator may do any of the following, or any combination of them:

(1)   meet the parties separately from each other or together and consider documents from one party not sent or shown to the other

(2)   conduct investigations in the absence of the parties

(3)   make use of specialist knowledge

(4)   obtain technical or legal advice

(5)   establish the procedures to be followed in the conciliation

13.1.6   The conciliator shall not be an arbitrator and the Arbitration Acts 1954 to 1998 and the law relating to arbitration shall not apply to the conciliation.

13.1.7   The conciliator's terms of appointment shall be those in the Works Requirements or, if there are none, those agreed by the Employer and the Contractor with the conciliator.

13.1.8   If the dispute is not resolved by agreement within 42 days after the conciliator was appointed, or a longer period proposed by the conciliator and agreed by the parties, the conciliator shall give both parties a written recommendation. The conciliator shall base the recommendation on the parties' rights and obligations under the Contract.

13.1.9   If either party is dissatisfied with the conciliator's recommendation, it may, within 45 days after receiving the conciliator's recommendation, so notify the other party. The notice shall state that it is given under sub-clause 13.1 of the Contract, and shall state the matters in dispute and the reasons for dissatisfaction. If the conciliator has failed to give a recommendation within 45 days after appointment, either party may give a notice of dissatisfaction. If notice of dissatisfaction has been given in accordance with this clause, either party may refer the dispute to arbitration under sub-clause 13.2.

13.1.10   If neither party gives notice of dissatisfaction within 45 days after receiving the conciliator's recommendation, the recommendation shall be conclusive and binding on the parties, and the parties agree to comply with it. If, in such circumstances, a party fails to comply with the conciliator's recommendation, the other party may [without limiting its other rights] refer the failure itself to arbitration under sub-clause 13.2, and need not invoke this sub-clause 13.1 for this reference.

13.1.11 If the conciliator has recommended the payment of money, even if a notice of dissatisfaction is given, the following shall apply:

(1) The party concerned shall make the payment recommended by the conciliator, provided that the other party first

(a) gave a notice, complying with the arbitration rules referred to in sub-clause 13.2, referring the same dispute to arbitration and

(b) gave the paying party a bond executed by a surety approved by the paying party, acting reasonably, in the form included in the Works Requirements, or if there is none, a form approved by the paying party, acting reasonably, for the amount of the payment.

(2) If, when the dispute is finally resolved, it is found that the party receiving payment on the conciliator's recommendation was not entitled to some or all of the amount paid, then that party shall repay the amount it was paid and found not to be entitled to, together with interest.

(3) When the dispute is finally resolved, interest will be deducted from final payment under the award or judgment.

(4) Interest under this sub-clause is calculated at the reference rate referred to in the European Communities (Late Payment in Commercial Transactions) Regulations 2002 plus 2% per year and runs from the date of the original payment to the date of the repayment or final payment.

(5) [This provision for interest is confidential under sub-clause 13.1.12, and in particular shall not be taken into account or referred to in arbitration until all other matters are resolved.]

13.1.12 The conciliation shall be confidential, and the parties shall respect its confidentiality, except when any of the exceptions in sub-clause 4.16 apply, or to the extent necessary to enforce a recommendation that has become conclusive and binding. All documents provided by a party in connection with a conciliation shall be returned when the conciliation is concluded.

13.2 Arbitration

Any dispute that, under sub-clause 13.1, may be referred to conciliation shall, subject to sub-clause 13.1 be finally settled by arbitration in accordance with the arbitration rules identified in the Schedule, part 1N. For purposes of those rules, the person or body to appoint the arbitrator, if not agreed by the parties, is named in the Schedule, part 1N.

13.3 Jurisdiction

Subject to the above provisions of this clause, the parties submit to the jurisdiction of the Irish courts to settle any dispute that may arise out of or in connection with the Contract or the Works.

13.4 Agent for Service

If an agent for service of legal proceedings on the Contractor is named in part 2A of the Schedule, the Contractor confirms to the Employer that it has irrevocably appointed the named person as its agent for the service of all documents relating to legal proceedings, and that failure of the agent to notify the Contractor of receipt of a document will not invalidate any proceedings or the service of the document.

13.5   Continuing obligations

[Despite the existence of a dispute, the parties shall continue to perform their obligations under the Contract.]

GENERAL COMMENTS ON CLAUSE 13

Any dispute can be referred to conciliation during the course of the Contract. The appointing body for the conciliator shall be described in the Schedule, Part 1, Section N. If the dispute is not resolved within 42 days after the appointment of the conciliator, the conciliator shall make his recommendation. The parties have 45 days to accept the recommendation.

If the recommendation stated that a sum of money should be paid by one party to the other then that shall be binding in the interim. The receiving party will have to provide a bond for the amount it receives.

If the recommendation is rejected by either party the matter can be referred to arbitration.

Any dispute referred to arbitration shall be subject to the arbitration rules stated in the Schedule, Part I, Section N.

End of Conditions.

OPTIONAL CLAUSES PV1 AND PV2

(Included in the Contract as stated in Schedule, part 1M)

PV1   PRICE VARIATION

PV1.1 Contract Sum Adjustment

The Contract Sum is adjusted for fluctuations in costs of resources only in respect of increases or decreases that occur in workers' wages or expenses, or material prices, or are made by Law, as follows:

PV1.1.1   Timing:

    (a) The **Base Date** means the first day of the 31st month after the Contract Date.

    (b) No increase or decrease that comes into being after the Date for Substantial Completion shall be taken into account for the purpose of this clause PV1.

PV1.1.2   Workers' wages and expenses

The Contract Sum shall be adjusted by the amount of an increase or decrease in workers' wages or expenses that satisfies all these requirements:

    (i) it is made to the standard normal and overtime hourly wage rates or expenses payable to workers according to the Labour Court's Registered Employment Agreement dated 15 March 1967 as varied from time to time under Section 28 of the Industrial Relations Act 1946 and

    (ii) it becomes payable after the Base Date in accordance with that agreement and

    (iii) it is in respect of General Round Increases conforming to the guidelines of the Social Partnership Agreements between the government, employer organisations and trade unions relating to such increases, or, in the absence of a Social Partnership Agreement and guidelines, increases in accordance with the guidelines on General Round Increases issued by the Department of Finance and

    (iv) the workers in respect of whom an increase is being claimed have received in Ireland for the relevant work at least the increased standard wage rates and expenses.

workers means

    (a) craftspersons and

    (b) semi-skilled and unskilled labour and

    (c) drivers and operators of plant and machinery and

    (d) time-keepers and clerical staff stationed on site and

    (e) any foreperson, charge hand or other person who supervises or administers while performing duties within (a)–(c), but in respect only of the standard wage rates according to sub-clause PV1.1.2(i) and expenses applicable to those duties and 50% of their total hours worked.

[Site agents, managers, other full time supervisors and administrators, and surveyors, for example, are excluded.]

General Round Increases means increases in workers' wages to the extent that they apply generally in the construction industry and are compliant with Government guidelines and Social Partnership Agreements.

expenses means expenses payable for country money and PRSI payable by the Contractor as employer.

[All other increases are excluded, even where calculated as a percentage of a standard rate. So, for example, the Contractor is not entitled to any payment for local or site bargaining provisions; any parity or restructuring increases; any bonus under a site agreement, productivity, incentive, or other bonus; insurance premiums, other on-costs or consequential costs].

PV1.1.3   Materials

The Contract Sum shall be adjusted by the amount of an increase or decrease in the Price of material that results from either or both of these calculations where applicable:

- So far as the Price of any material at the Purchase Date has increased by more than 50 percent of the Price at the first business day of the month in which the purchase occurred or the Price at the Designated Date (whichever is highest) then that excess percentage over 50 percent is applied to its Price at the Designated Date.

- So far as the Price of any material at the Base Date has increased or decreased at the Purchase Date by more than 10 percent, then that excess percentage over 10 percent is applied to the Price at the Base Date.

material means only

(a)   material invoiced to the project

(b)   for incorporation in the permanent Works [as fixtures or unfixed goods],

(c)   or for temporary works used on the Site

(d)   and not used on any previous project or usable on any subsequent one [for example, replaceable components in formwork]. [Tools or equipment are not 'material'. There is no deduction of normal wastage from the allowable quantity of material, or of extra or surplus material taken over by the Employer].

Purchase Date means the date when the particular material was invoiced to the project.

Price means the average price at which the relevant volume of the relevant material is available in the market at the relevant time from a representative number of reputable manufacturers or suppliers.

[There is no adjustment for any alteration in the price of material except as specified in this sub-clause].

PV1.1.4   Law

The Contract Sum shall be adjusted by the amount of any increase or decrease in the Contractor's cost of performing its obligations under the Contract as a result of a change in Law made after the Designated Date that

(i)   changes [whether by alteration, addition or removal] Value Added Tax, excise duty or tariff, requirements for a licence to import or export any commodity or Pay-Related Social Insurance and

(ii)   is not identified in the Works Requirements and

(iii)   has not resulted in an adjustment in the Contract Sum under another part of this clause PV1 or the Contract.

PV1.2   Communications

The Contractor shall maintain arrangements to become aware of any significant possibility of an increase or decrease in the Contract Sum that may arise in accordance with this clause PV1 and shall immediately notify the Employer's Representative of any such possibility and keep him informed of any opportunities to minimise an increase.

PV1.3 Compensation Events

The Pricing Document and the valuation rules in sub-clause 10.6 shall not cease to determine, apply to or be the basis of the valuation of a Compensation Event by reason of price fluctuations in material costs, but the following principles shall apply –

(i)   No departure from rates in the Pricing Document shall be made in respect of fluctuations affecting the cost of material omitted by a Change Order.

(ii) Valuation of a Change Order shall include any increase in the cost to the Contractor of material substituted or added by the Change Order that is due to price fluctuation after the Designated Date so far as it is likely to exceed the price fluctuation increase that under this clause PV1 would have been the Contractor's risk for the original material.

No adjustment under this clause PV1 shall apply to an adjustment or the part of an adjustment of the Contract Sum valued under sub-clauses 10.6.4 or 10.7.

PV1.4 Efficiency

[In addition to sub-clause PV1.1.1(b),] increases of the Contract Sum will only apply so far as the increased costs incurred by the Contractor occur despite its efficient progress and procurement and reasonable efforts to minimise increases.

PV1.5 Certificates & payment

The Contractor shall fully detail and vouch any fluctuations in costs relevant to this clause PV1 as soon as practicable, and they shall then be allowed for in interim and final certificates and payments under and subject to clause 11.

PV2 PRICE VARIATION

PV2.1 Definitions

For the purpose of this clause definitions are set out in Appendix 1 [as well as elsewhere in the Conditions]. References to Appendices 2 and 3 are to the completed Appendices 2 and 3 in the Pricing Document, if they are there.

PV2.2 Contract Sum Adjustment

The Contract Sum, excluding the amount of Non-Adjustable Overheads, shall be subject to adjustment for price fluctuations or changes in Law only in the circumstances set out in this clause PV2. No increase or decrease shall be made in respect of any amount that relates to works before the Base Date except as provided in sub-clauses PV2.4 and PV2.8.4.

PV2.3 Proportions

For the purpose of calculating adjustments to the Contract Sum, the proportions of Labour, Materials, Fuel, Non-Reusable Temporary Works, and Non-Adjustable Overheads in the Contract Sum are set out in Appendix 2 [irrespective of the actual proportions of the work].

PV2.4 Change in Law

The Contract Sum shall be adjusted by the amount of any increase or decrease in the Contractor's cost of performing its obligations under the Contract as a result of a change in Law made after the Designated Date, or if a Recovery date has been agreed or determined, made after the Recovery Date, but before the Date for Substantial Completion of the Works or a Section, that

(i) changes [whether by alteration, addition or removal] Value Added Tax, excise duty or tariff, requirements for a licence to import or export any commodity or Pay-Related Social Insurance and

(ii) is not identified in the Works Requirements and

(iii) has not resulted in an adjustment in the Contract Sum under another part of this clause PV2 or the Contract.

PV2.5 Failure to complete on time

If the Contractor fails to complete the Works or a Section by its Date for Substantial Completion, adjustment of the Contract Sum in respect of the Works or Section after its Date for Substantial Completion shall be effected by the Index Figures, General Round Increases or Consumer Price Index applicable to the Adjustment Period in which the Date for Substantial Completion occurs.

PV2.6 Excluded Amounts

The following are not subject to price adjustment (**Excluded Amounts**):

(a) Delay cost under sub-clause 10.7

(b) Adjustments or parts of adjustments of the Contract Sum valued under sub-clause 10.6.4

(c) Amounts for unfixed materials or goods for which the Contractor is entitled to payment under sub-clause 11.2

(d) Amounts based on actual costs or current prices

(e) Credits allowed for old materials arising from the Works

(f)   Amounts for work executed under an agreement containing specific price arrangements

(g)   Costs incurred for making good defects under clause 8

(h)   [In addition to sub-clause PV2.5] amounts by which any cost incurred by the Contractor has been increased by a default of the Contractor.

PV2.7   Revisions of Index Figures

If an Index Figure used for a Material Category or a Fuel Category or the Consumer Price Index in relation to Non-Reusable Temporary Works is subsequently revised by the Central Statistics Office prior to the issue of the Final Certificate, any adjustments in accordance with this Clause shall be recalculated on the basis of the revised Index Figures.

PV2.8   Materials and Fuel

PV2.8.1   Weightings

For the purpose of calculating any adjustments to the amount payable in respect of Materials and Fuel in an Interim or Final Certificate, the weightings of Material and Fuel Categories in the Contract Sum are set out in Part I or Part II of Appendix 3, as applicable [irrespective of the actual constituents, weightings or proportions of the work].

PV2.8.2   Materials

Subject to sub-clause PV2.8.4, the amount payable in respect of Materials in an Interim Certificate or in the Final Certificate (other than amounts for price adjustments under this clause PV2 or any Excluded Amounts) in respect of an Adjustment Period shall be increased or decreased in accordance with the provisions of this clause PV2, and the total adjustment to the amount payable in such Interim Certificate or in the Final Certificate in respect of Materials shall be equal to the sum of the adjustments for each Material Category, which adjustments shall be calculated using the relevant formula set out in Appendix 4.

PV2.8.3   Fuel

Subject to sub-clause PV2.8.4, the amount payable in respect of the Fuel Percentage of an Interim Certificate or of the Final Certificate (other than amounts for price adjustments under this clause PV2 or any Excluded Amounts) in respect of an Adjustment Period shall be increased or decreased in accordance with the provisions of this clause PV2, and the total adjustment to the amount payable in such Interim Certificate or in the Final Certificate in respect of the Fuel Percentage shall be equal to the sum of the adjustments for each Fuel Category, which adjustments shall be calculated using the relevant formula set out in Appendix 5.

PV2.8.4   Exceptional Increases for Materials and Fuel

The amount payable in respect of a Material and/or the Fuel Percentage in an Interim Certificate or in the Final Certificate (other than amounts for price adjustments under this clause PV2 or any Excluded Amounts) may be increased for any Exceptional Increase in respect of that Material and/or Fuel after the Designated Date, or, if a Recovery Date has been agreed or determined, after the Recovery Date calculated using the relevant formula for Materials or Fuel set out in Appendix 6, as appropriate, **provided however** that adjustment of the Contract Sum under this sub-clause in respect of works after the Base Date shall be effected by the greater of the increase calculated in accordance with this sub-clause PV2.8.4 and the relevant increase calculated in accordance with sub-clause PV2.8.2 in respect of that Material or in accordance with sub-clause PV2.8.3 in respect of that Fuel.

PV2.8.5   Non-Reusable Temporary Works

The amount payable in respect of Non-Reusable Temporary Works in an Interim Certificate or the Final Certificate (other than amounts for price adjustments under this clause PV2 or any Excluded Amounts) issued in respect of an Adjustment Period shall be adjusted in accordance with the relevant formula set out in Appendix 7.

PV2.8.6   Labour

The amount payable in respect of Labour in an Interim Certificate or the Final Certificate (other than amounts for price adjustments under this clause PV2 or any Excluded Amounts) issued in respect of an Adjustment Period shall be adjusted in accordance with the relevant formula set out in Appendix 8, **but only** to the extent that the workers in respect of whom an increase is being claimed have received in Ireland for the relevant work at least the increased standard wage rates.

Appendix 1 to Clause PV2

Definitions

(a) **Adjustment Index Figure** means the appropriate Index Figure for the Adjustment Month **provided however** that, the Index Figure for any Adjustment Month that occurs after the Date for Substantial Completion of the Works or a relevant Section shall be determined in accordance with sub-clause PV2.5.

(b) **Adjustment Month** means the month during which the middle day of the Adjustment Period occurred (if the Adjustment Period is an even number of days the last day is not to be counted).

(c) **Adjustment Period** means the period between the last preceding Interim Certificate and the current Interim Certificate or the Final Certificate, **provided however** that if any Certificate is calculated in respect of a period that includes works before and after the Base Date, then only that part of the period that falls after the Base Date will be the Adjustment Period for the purposes of that certificate.

(d) **Base Date** means the first day of the 37th calendar month after the Designated Date, or if a Recovery Date has been agreed or determined, after the Recovery Date.

(e) **Base Index Figure** means the appropriate Index Figure for the Base Month.

(f) **Base Month** means the month during which the Base Date occurs.

(g) **Category** means any Material Category or Non-Reusable Temporary Works.

(h) **Consumer Price Index** means the consumer price index (all items) published by the Central Statistics Office, Ireland (including any successor or replacement thereof).

(i) **Effective Value** is the difference between

  (I) the amount which is due in any Interim or Final Certificate (before deducting retention) less any amounts for price adjustments and Excluded Amounts

and

  (II) the amount included in the last preceding Interim Certificate calculated in accordance with (I) above **provided that** in the case of the first Interim Certificate the Effective Value shall be the amount calculated in accordance with (I) above,

  provided however that if any amount payable in any Interim or Final Certificate is calculated in respect of works before the Base Date, then only that part of the amount payable in such Interim or Final Certificate that refers to works after the Base Date (less any amounts for price adjustments and any Excluded Amounts) will be included in the Effective Value, except that works before the Base Date may be included in the Effective Value for the purposes only of sub-clause PV2.8.4.

(j) **Exceptional Increase** means that part of an increase that is in excess of 50% from one CSO monthly Index Figure to the next CSO monthly Index Figure for a particular Material or Fuel Category after the Designated Date or, if a Recovery Date has been agreed or determined after the Recovery Date to the extent that such increase is in excess of 50% above the CSO monthly Index Figure for that Material or Fuel Category at the Designated Date or, if a Recovery Date has been agreed or determined, at the Recovery Date.

(k) **Final Certificate** means a certificate provided by the Employer's Representative in accordance with sub-clause 11.5.3.

(l) **Fuel** and **Fuel Category** means any or all of the sources of energy listed in Part II of Appendix 3, as appropriate.

(m) **Fuel Percentage** means the percentage of the Contract Sum that consists of Fuel set out in Appendix 2.

(n) **General Round Increase** means increases in workers' wages to the extent that they apply to all workers in the construction industry and are compliant with Government guidelines and Social Partnership Agreements.

[All other increases are excluded, even where calculated as a percentage of a standard rate. So, for example, the Contractor is not entitled to any payment for local or site bargaining provisions; any parity or restructuring increases; any bonus under a site agreement, productivity, incentive, or other bonus; PRSI, insurance premiums, or other on-costs or consequential costs.]

(o) **Index Figures** means those index figures compiled by or on behalf of the Central Statistics Office, Ireland (or such other public body as is authorised to perform this function) applicable to each Material or Fuel Category listed in Appendix 3, or, where appropriate, Consumer Price Index figures.

(p) **Interim Certificate** means a certificate or penultimate payment certificate provided by the Employer's Representative in accordance with sub-clause 11.1.3 or sub-clause 11.5.2.

(q) **Labour Percentage** means the percentage of the Contract Sum that consists of Labour set out in Appendix 2.

(r) **Material(s)** and **Material Category** means any or all of the materials listed in Part I of Appendix 3, as appropriate.

(s) **Materials Percentage** means the percentage of the Contract Sum that consists of Materials set out in Appendix 2.

(t) **Non-Adjustable Overheads** means the percentage of the Contract Sum that consists of non-adjustable overheads set out in Appendix 2.

(u) **Non-Reusable Temporary Works** means those Work Elements identified in the Pricing Document or Works Requirements as being non-reusable temporary works.

(v) **Non-Reusable Temporary Works Percentage** means the percentage of the Contract Sum that consists of non-reusable temporary works set out in Appendix 2.

(w) **Recovery Date** means the Designated Date adjusted by the period of delay to the Starting Date that results from the actions or omissions of the Contractor after the Contract Date, but prior to the Starting Date (the **Contractor's Period of Delay**) as is agreed by the parties. If the parties do not agree the Recovery Date then the Employer may deliver to the Employer's Representative full and detailed particulars of any claim to a Contractor's Period of Delay and the Recovery Date shall be the Designated Date adjusted by the Contractor's Period of Delay, if any, that the Employer's Representative certifies as fair and reasonable.

(x) **Work Element** means a constituent of the work in the Pricing Document, or such other tender document as appropriate, for which the Employer's Representative has identified a corresponding Material Category or that forms part of the Non-Reusable Temporary Works, and which is not an Excluded Amount, **provided however** that no work before the Base Date shall form part of a Work Element for the purposes of adjustment in accordance with this Clause, with the exception of sub-clause PV2.8.4.

Appendix 2 to Clause PV2

Proportions of Labour, Materials, Fuel, Non-reusable Temporary Works, Plant and Non-adjustable Overheads

	Works	Amount (Euro)	Percentage of Contract Sum
(a)	Labour		——%
(b)	Materials		——%
(c)	Fuel		——%
(d)	Non-Reusable Temporary Works		——%
(f)	Non-Adjustable Overheads		——%
	Totals		**100%**

Appendix 3 to Clause PV2

Indices And Weightings For Materials And Fuel

Part 1:   Indices and weightings for Material Categories

In respect of the **Materials** identified below the following proportions apply and the total of such proportions shall amount to a factor of one (1):

Extract from Central Statistics Office Data – Table 3A

Wholesale Price Indices (excluding VAT) for Building and Construction Materials

	Weightings	Materials
(1)	0.	Stone, sand and gravel
(1.1)	0.	Stone
(1.2)	0.	Sand and Gravel
(2)	0.	Cement
(3)	0.	Ready Mixed Mortar and Concrete
(4)	0.	Concrete Blocks and Bricks
(5)	0.	Other Concrete Products
(5.1)	0.	Precast Concrete
(6)	0.	Structural Steel and Reinforcing Metal
(6.1)	0.	Structural Steel
(6.2)	0.	Fabricated Metal
(6.3)	0.	Reinforcing Metal
(6.4)	0.	Other Steel Products
(7)	0.	Rough Timber (including plain sawn)
(7.1)	0.	Hardwood
(7.2)	0.	Rough Timber
(8)	0.	Other Timber
(8.1)	0.	Windows and Doors
(9)	0.	Bituminous macadam, asphalt and bituminous emulsions of which
(9.1)	0.	Bituminous macadam and asphalt
(9.2)	0.	Bituminous emulsions
(10)	0.	Electrical Fittings
(10.1)	0.	Lighting Equipment
(10.2)	0.	Protection and Communication Equipment
(11)	0.	All other materials
(11.1)	0.	Plumbing Materials including Sanitary ware
(11.2)	0.	HVAC (Heating and Ventilation Equipment)
(11.3)	0.	Insulating Materials
(11.4)	0.	Pipes and Fittings
(11.4.1)	0.	PVC
(11.4.2)	0.	Copper
(11.5)	0.	Plaster
(11.6)	0.	Paints, oils and varnishes
(11.7)	0.	Glass
(11.8)	0.	All other metal fittings
(11.9)	0.	All other products

Part 2:   Indices and weightings for Fuel Categories

In respect of the **Fuel** identified below the following proportions apply and the total of such proportions shall amount to a factor of one (1):

	Extract from Central Statistics Office Data – Table 5	
	Wholesale Price Indices (excluding VAT) for Energy Products (i.e. Fuels purchased by Manufacturing Industry)	
	Weightings	**Materials**
(1)	0.	Fuel Oil
(2)	0.	Electricity
(3)	0.	Gas
Total	**1.00**	

Appendix 4 to Clause PV2

Materials

The formulae for price fluctuations in Material Categories pursuant to sub-clause PV2.8.2 are as follows:

A. **Formula to be used where A1 – B1 is less than or equal to zero:**

$$W \times Y \times Z \times P \times \frac{(A1 - B1)}{B1} = K$$

B. **Formula to be used where A1 – B1 is greater than zero:**

$$\left\{ W \times Y \times Z \times P \times \frac{(A1 - B1)}{B1} \right\} - (10\% \times W \times Y \times Z \times P) = K$$

PROVIDED THAT if K under Formula B is less than zero for the relevant Material Category solely as a result of the deduction of the ten percent (10%), the adjustment for that Material Category shall be zero.

(*Note: Formula B will deduct 10% from any increase in the indices and effectively sets Base Index + 10% as the threshold at which recovery starts.*)

where:

W = The weighting attributed to a particular Material Category, as stated in Part I of Appendix 3.

Y = The Materials Percentage.

Z = Contract Sum (excluding VAT and any price adjustments under this Clause) less any Excluded Amounts.

P = The amount which is due in any Interim or Final Certificate for the relevant Material Category less the last amount, if any, for that Material Category included in an Interim Certificate with the resulting balance divided by the total amount for that Material Category in the Contract Sum **provided that** the aggregate value of P in respect of any Material Category calculated over the course of the contract shall not exceed 1. In the calculation of P all amounts relating to price adjustments under this Clause shall be excluded.

The amounts in the Interim Certificates and/or Final Certificate used to calculate this proportion P are those for Work Elements allocated to the relevant Material Category in the Pricing Document or other pricing document forming part of the Contract.

No amount for a Work Element (or part of a Work Element) in the Pricing Document, or other pricing document forming part of the Contract may be used for the calculation of adjustments for more than one Category.

A1 = The Adjustment Index Figure for the relevant Material Category.

B1 = The Base Index Figure for the relevant Material Category.

K = The amount of increase or decrease recoverable in relation to price fluctuations for the particular Material in an Interim or Final Certificate.

Provided however that if at any time the Central Statistics Office ceases to publish Index Figures in respect of a particular Material Category then the following formula shall apply for calculating any increases or decreases in respect of that Material in any Interim Certificate and/or Final Certificate issued in respect of works after such time **provided always** that any such increases or decreases shall only apply in respect of works after the Base Date:

A. **Formula to be used where CPI^A – CPI^B is less than or equal to zero:**

$$W \times Y \times Z \times P \times \frac{(CPI^A - CPI^B)}{CPI^B} = K$$

B. **Formula to be used where CPI^A – CPI^B is greater than zero:**

$$\left\{ W \times Y \times Z \times P \times \frac{(CPI^A - CPI^B)}{CPI^B} \right\} - (10\% \times W \times Y \times Z \times P) = K$$

PROVIDED THAT if K under Formula B is less than zero for the relevant Material Category solely as a result of the deduction of the ten percent (10%), the adjustment for that Material Category shall be zero.

where:

CPI^A = the Consumer Price Index for the Adjustment Month.

CPI^B = the Consumer Price Index for the Base Month.

Worked Example:

A four year contract is in its 44th month and material price increases occurring after the expiry of the 37th month (i.e. after the Base Date) are claimable in Interim Valuations. The 43rd Interim Valuation has included in it a claim for an increase in the price of ready mixed mortar and concrete which occurred after the Base Date.

The Contract Sum (excluding VAT and any price adjustments under this Clause) less any Excluded Amounts is €6,000,000 ("Z").

The percentage of the contract sum (excluding VAT) attributable to Materials ("Y") is 35%.

The weighting for ready mixed mortar and concrete in the tender documents ("W") is 20%.

Index Figures:

The Base Index Figure is 105.3.

The Adjustment Index Figure is 126.36.

The recoverable increase is calculated as follows:

W = Ready mixed mortar and concrete weighting is 0.2 as stated in Appendix 3.

Y = 35% as stated in Appendix 2.

Z = €6,000,000.

P = The proportion of the particular Material Category in the Contract Sum (prior to any adjustments) as accepted by the Employer's Representative being paid for in the Interim Valuation (as certified) is 25% (this percentage is arrived at by calculating the difference between the amount due in the Interim or Final Certificate for the relevant Material Category less the last amount, if any, for that Material Category in an Interim Certificate with the resulting balance divided by the total amount of that Material Category in the Contract Sum).

A1 = The Adjustment Index Figure for ready mixed mortar and concrete is 126.36.

B1 = The Base Index Figure for ready mixed mortar and concrete is 105.3.

K = The amount of increase or decrease recoverable.

$$\left\{ W \times Y \times Z \times P \times \frac{(A1 - B1)}{B1} \right\} - (10\% \times W \times Y \times Z \times P) = K$$

$$\left\{ .2 \times .35 \times 6,000,000 \times .25 \times \frac{(126.36 - 105.3)}{105.3} \right\} - (10\% \times .2 \times .35 \times 6,000,000 \times .25) = €10,500$$

The amount of the recoverable increase for ready mixed mortar and concrete is €10,500

(*This €10,500 will be added to the recoverable increase for other materials in order to determine the overall increase for materials in this certificate.*)

Appendix 5 to Clause PV2

Fuel

The formulae for price fluctuations in Fuel Categories pursuant to sub-clause PV2.8.3 are as follows:

A. **Formula to be used where A1 – B1 is less than or equal to zero:**

$$W \times Y \times EV \times \frac{(A1 - B1)}{B1} = L$$

B. **Formula to be used where A1 – B1 is greater than zero:**

$$\left\{ W \times Y \times EV \times \frac{(A1 - B1)}{B1} \right\} - (10\% \times W \times Y \times EV) = L$$

PROVIDED THAT if L under (B) above is less than zero for the relevant Fuel Category solely as a result of the deduction of the ten percent (10%), the adjustment for that Fuel Category shall be zero.

where:

W = The weighting attributed to a particular Fuel Category, as stated in Part II of Appendix 3.

Y = The Fuel Percentage.

EV = Effective Value (excluding VAT).

A1 = The Adjustment Index Figure for the relevant Fuel Category.

B1 = The Base Index Figure for the relevant Fuel Category.

L = The amount of increase or decrease recoverable in relation to price fluctuations in the particular Fuel Category in an Interim or Final Certificate.

Provided however that if at any time the Central Statistics Office ceases to publish Index Figures in respect of a particular Fuel Category then the following formula shall apply for calculating any increases or decreases in respect of that Fuel in any Interim Certificate and/or Final Certificate issued in respect of works after such time **provided always** that any such increases or decreases shall only apply in respect of works after the Base Date:

A. **Formula to be used where $CPI^A - CPI^B$ is less than or equal to zero:**

$$W \times Y \times EV \times \frac{(CPI^A - CPI^B)}{CPI^B} = L$$

B. **Formula to be used where $A1 - CPI^B$ is greater than zero:**

$$\left\{ W \times Y \times EV \times \frac{(CPI^A - CPI^B)}{CPI^B} \right\} - (10\% \times W \times Y \times EV) = L$$

PROVIDED THAT if L under Formula B is less than zero for the relevant Fuel Category solely as a result of the deduction of the ten percent (10%), the adjustment for that Fuel Category shall be zero.

where:

CPI^A = the Consumer Price Index for the Adjustment Month, subject to sub-clause PV2.5.

CPI^B = the Consumer Price Index for the Base Month.

Appendix 6 to Clause PV2

Exceptional Increases Under Sub-Clause PV2.8.4

Part I: Materials

The formula for exceptional increases in respect of any Material Category pursuant to sub-clause PV2.8.4 is:

Formula to be used where F2 is greater than or equal to D1 plus 50% and greater than F1 plus 50%:

$$\left[W \times Y \times Z \times P \times \frac{(F2 - F1)}{F1} \right] - (50\% \times W \times Y \times Z \times P) = M$$

where:

W = W as defined in Appendix 4.

Y = Y as defined in Appendix 4.

Z = Z as defined in Appendix 4.

P = P as defined in Appendix 4.

$D1$ = the Index Figure corresponding to the relevant Material Category at the Designated Date or, if a Recovery Date has been agreed or determined, at the Recovery Date.

$F1$ = the Index Figure corresponding to the relevant Material Category in the month preceding the month during which the middle day of the period during which the works occurred that correspond to the relevant Interim Certificate or the Final Certificate falls **provided however** that if the Date for Substantial Completion of the Works or a relevant Section falls in or after this month there shall be no adjustment to the Contract Sum.

$F2$ = the Index Figure for the relevant Material Category applicable at the middle day of the period during which the works occurred that correspond to the relevant Interim Certificate or the Final Certificate, **provided however** that if any Certificate is calculated in respect of a period that includes works after the Date for Substantial Completion of the Works or a relevant Section, then the Index Figure in respect of the works after relevant Date for Substantial Completion shall be the Index Figure for that Material Category at that Date for Substantial Completion.

M = the amount of the increase recoverable under sub-clause PV2.8.4 in respect of a particular Material Category in an Interim or Final Certificate.

Part II: Fuel

The formula for exceptional increases in respect of any Fuel Category pursuant to sub-clause PV2.8.4 is:

Formula to be used where F1 is greater than or equal to D1 plus 50% and also greater than F1 plus 50%:

$$\left[W \times Y \times EV \times \frac{(F2 - F1)}{F1} \right] - (50\% \times W \times Y \times EV) = N$$

where:

W = W as defined in Appendix 5.

Y = Y as defined in Appendix 5.

EV = EV as defined in Appendix 5.

$D1$ = the Index Figure corresponding to the relevant Fuel Category at the Designated Date or, if a Recovery Date has been agreed or determined, at the Recovery Date.

$F1$ = the Index Figure corresponding to the relevant Fuel Category in the month preceding the month in which the middle day of the period during which the works occurred that correspond to the relevant Interim Certificate or the Final Certificate falls **provided however** that if the Date for Substantial Completion of the Works or a relevant Section falls in or after this month there shall be no adjustment to the Contract Sum.

$F2 =$ the Index Figure for the relevant Fuel Category applicable at the middle day of the period during which the works occurred that correspond to the relevant Interim Certificate or the Final Certificate, **provided however** that if any Certificate is calculated in respect of a period that includes works after the Date for Substantial Completion of the Works or a relevant Section, then the Index Figure in respect of the works after the relevant Date for Substantial Completion shall be the Index Figure for that Fuel Category at that Date for Substantial Completion.

$N =$ the amount of the exceptional increase recoverable under sub-clause PV2.8.4 in respect of a particular Fuel Category in an Interim or Final Certificate.

Appendix 7 to Clause PV2

Non-Reusable Temporary Works

The formulae for price fluctuations in Non-Reusable Temporary Works are as follows:

A. **Formula to be used where $\dfrac{CPI^A - CPI^B}{CPI^B}$ is less than or equal to zero:**

$$Y \times Z \times P \times \frac{(CPI^A - CPI^B)}{CPI^B} = K$$

B. **Formula to be used where $\dfrac{CPI^A - CPI^B}{CPI^B}$ is greater than zero:**

$$\left\{ Y \times Z \times P \times \frac{(CPI^A - CPI^B)}{CPI^B} \right\} - (10\% \times Y \times Z \times P) = K$$

PROVIDED THAT if K under Formula B is less than zero for Non-Reusable Temporary Works solely as a result of the deduction of the ten percent (10%), the adjustment for Non-Reusable Temporary Works shall be zero.

(*Note: Formula B will deduct 10% from any increase in the indices and effectively sets Base Index + 10% as the threshold at which recovery starts.*)

where:

Y = The Non-Reusable Temporary Works Percentage.

Z = Z as defined in Appendix 4.

P = The amount which is due in any Interim or Final Certificate for Non-Reusable Temporary Works less the last amount, if any, for Non-Reusable Temporary Works included in an Interim Certificate with the resulting balance divided by the total amount for Non-Reusable Temporary Works in the Contract Sum provided the aggregate value of P in respect of any Non-Reusable Temporary Works calculated over the course of the contract shall not exceed 1. In the calculation of "P" all amounts relating to the recovery of price adjustments shall be excluded.

The amounts in the Interim Certificates and/or Final Certificate used to calculate this proportion "P" are those for Work Elements allocated to Non-Reusable Temporary Works in the Pricing Document or other pricing document forming part of the Contract.

No amount for a Work Element (or part of a Work Element) in the Pricing Document, or other pricing document forming part of the Contract may be used for the calculation of adjustments for more than one Category.

Appendix 8 to Clause PV2

Labour

The formula for **Labour Variations (LV)** pursuant to sub-clause PV2.8.6 is:

$$LV = Y \times GRI \times EV$$

where:

LV = The amount of increase or decrease recoverable in respect of Labour in an Interim or Final Certificate.

Y = The Labour Percentage.

GRI = The currently applicable General Round Increase expressed as a percentage. Only General Round Increases coming into effect after the Base Date and prior to the Date for Substantial Completion of the Works or a relevant Section shall be applicable. Where there are two or more General Round Increases that apply concurrently, the average General Round Increase shall apply.

General Round Increases exclude any increase in workers' wages that exceeds the percentage increases in basic pay in the private sector as agreed in the current Social Partnership Agreement.

EV = Effective Value (excluding VAT).

Provided however that if there is no Social Partnership Agreement or government guidelines in effect during the relevant Adjustment Period the following formula shall apply for calculating Labour Variations in lieu of General Round Increases:

$$LV = \frac{(CPI^A - CPI^B)}{CPI^B} \times Y \times EV$$

where:

CPI^A = the Consumer Price Index for the Adjustment Month.

CPI^B = the Consumer Price Index for the Base Month.

SCHEDULE

PART 1
(Completed by the Employer before Tender)

A Employer's Representative and Communications
Sub-clauses 4.3 *and* 4.14

Details for sending notices under clauses 12 and 13 to the Employer are

For the attention of ....
Address
....
....
....

Details for sending other notices to the Employer are

For the attention of ....
Address
....
....
....
fax ....
email ....

The Employer's Representative is ....

Details for sending notices to the Employer's Representative are

For the attention of ....
Address
....
....
....
fax ....
email ....

Limitations on the Employer's Representative's authority to perform its functions and powers under the Contract

- Maximum adjustment to the Contract Sum for a single Change Order €..............................., unless approved by the Employer

- Maximum cumulative value of adjustments to the Contract Sum for Change Orders in any 3 month period €......................., unless approved by the Employer

- The Employer's Representative shall not make a Change Order causing or contributing to a reduction in safety, scope, quality or usefulness of the Works without the Employer's approval

- The Employer will decide whether to accept or reject a value engineering proposal

- The Employer must agree to reduce retention if the Defects Period is extended

- The Employer's Representative is to consult with the Employer in relation to any adjustment to the Contract Sum before determining the adjustment

- Where the Employer has appointed a quantity surveyor, the Employer's Representative is to consult with the quantity surveyor in relation to any adjustments to the Contract Sum before determining the adjustment

- ....

- ....

NOTE

Section A provides details for communications with the Employer for notices in connection with clauses 12 (Termination) and 13 (Disputes). This part also provides the name and address of the Employer's Representative and Limitations of the Employer's Representative. The limitations are:

    (i)   A maximum value of a Change Order, unless approved by the Employer;

    (ii)   A maximum number of Change Orders in any three-month period with a cumulative value of € (to be stated), unless approved by the Employer;

    (iii)   A Change Order shall not cause or contribute to any reduction in safety, scope, quality or usefulness of the Works without the approval of the Employer;

    (iv)   The Employer's Representative must consult the Employer before determining any adjustment to the Contract Sum;

    (v)   Where a quantity surveyor is appointed, the Employer's Representative will consult the quantity surveyor before determining any adjustment to the Contract Sum;

    (vi)   Other limitations may be specified by the Employer.

B Documents

The **Works Requirements** are

....

....

....

....

The **Pricing Document** is

....

....

....

....

NOTE

This part will contain details of the Works Requirements as set out by the Employer, the Pricing Document and, if there is a Bill of Quantities, the method of measurement under which the bills were prepared.

   It will be stated in Part K (Item 17) of the Schedule whether quantities do or do not form part of the Contract.

C Property in Contractor's Documents
Sub-clause 6.4

Ownership in Contractor's Documents and Works Proposals described in sub-clause 6.4.2 does/does not transfer to the Employer in accordance with sub-clause 6.4. (If neither deleted, read as 'does not'.)

NOTE

Sub-clause 6.4.2 provides the Employer with the opportunity of taking ownership of the copyright of all documents and Works Proposals. The Employer must state whether or not he wishes to exercise this option in the Schedule. In the event that the Employer wishes to take ownership of copyright then the Contractor is obliged to transfer the copyright to the Employer. The agreement of all subcontractors, suppliers and designers must be secured at tender/order stage.

D Insurance
Clause 3

Insurance of the Works: minimum amount insured for professional fees .... % of the Contract Sum (if none stated, 12½%)

Minimum indemnity limits for public liability and employers' liability insurance:

- public liability insurance: €................................ for any one event, but this limit may be on an annual aggregate basis for products liability, collapse, vibration, subsidence, removal and weakening of supports and sudden and accidental pollution. (If not stated, €6,500,000.)

- employers' liability insurance: €................................ for any one event. (If not stated, €13,000,000.)

Maximum excess for Insurance:

- insurance of Works and other Risk Items: €................................ (If not stated, €10,000.)

- public liability: €.............................. in respect of property damage only (If not stated, €10,000). There shall be no excess for death, injury or illness.

- employers' liability: no excess.

Permitted exclusions from the Insurances:

- permitted exclusions from all Insurances:
  - war, invasion, act of foreign enemies, hostilities [whether war is declared or not], civil war, rebellion, revolution, insurrection or military or usurped power
  - pressure waves caused by aircraft or other airborne objects travelling at sonic or supersonic speeds
  - contamination by radioactivity or radioactive, toxic, explosive or other hazardous properties of any explosive nuclear assembly or its components, in each case not caused by the Contractor or the Contractor's Personnel
  - terrorism (*delete if terrorism insurance is required*)
  - asbestos (*delete if asbestos insurance is required*)

- permitted exclusions from insurance of the Works and other Risk Items:
  - use or occupation of the Works by the Employer except in connection with the Works
  - unless otherwise specified in the Works Requirements, cost of making good defects in the Works but not damage caused by such defects to other sound parts of the Works
  - wear, tear, normal upkeep or normal repair or gradual deterioration
  - inventory losses
  - loss of use or any consequential loss of any nature including penalties for delay, non-completion or non-compliance
  - failure of information technology
  - mechanical or electrical breakdown but not resulting damage
  - cessation of the Works for more than 3 months

- permitted exclusions from public liability insurance:
  - persons under a contract of service or apprenticeship with the insured
  - property of the insured or in the insured's custody or control other than existing premises and their contents temporarily occupied for the purposes of the Works

- o defective workmanship or materials but not resulting damage

- o mechanically propelled vehicles within the meaning of the Road Traffic Acts

- o loss or damage due to design/design for a fee/defective workmanship, materials or design but including its consequences (*delete two*. If two not deleted, permitted exclusion is "loss or damage due to design".)

- o gradual pollution or contamination

- o territorial limits

- o unless otherwise specified in the Works Requirements, aircraft and waterborne craft

- o fines, penalties, liquidated damages

- • permitted exclusions from employer's liability insurance:

- o offshore work

- o liability compulsorily insurable under the Road Traffic Acts

- • permitted exclusions from professional indemnity insurance

- o Persons under a contract of service or apprenticeship with the insured

- o Ownership, use, occupation or leasing of mobile or immobile property

- o Effecting or maintenance of insurance of or in connection with the provision of finance or advice on financial matters

- o Dishonest, malicious, criminal or deliberate illegal acts

- o Libel and slander

- o Insolvency

- o Fines, penalties, liquidated damages or any penal, punitive, exemplary, non-compensatory or aggravated damages

- o Failure of information technology

- o Contractual liability that would not apply in the absence of the contract

Optional insurance provisions:

The Employer shall/shall not have the risk of loss of and damage to its existing facilities and parts of the Works it uses or occupies, in accordance with sub-clause 3.8. (*Delete as applicable*. If none deleted, the Employer shall not have this risk, and sub-clause 3.8 shall not apply.)

Insurance of the Works and other Risk Items shall include the following property of the Employer, other than the Works and Works Items:
....
and the minimum sum for which this property is to be insured shall be €...............................

If Insurance of the Works and other Risk Items is to include terrorism cover, the minimum sum insured shall be €..............................

The Contractor shall/is not required to (*delete one*) extend the insurance of the Works and other Risk Items for a Section that has reached Substantial Completion until the Employer's Representative issues the certificate of Substantial Completion for the whole Works.

Required extensions to Insurance:
....

Professional indemnity insurance is/is not (*delete one*) required. (If neither deleted, professional indemnity insurance is not required.) If required, the professional indemnity insurance is to be kept in place for .... years after Substantial Completion of the Works is certified by the Employer's Representative. If required, the minimum indemnity limit for professional indemnity insurance shall be €...................... for each and every claim or series of claims arising from the same originating cause/annual aggregate limit (*delete one*). The maximum excess shall be €..................... (If none stated, €50,000.)

> **NOTE**
>
> Contractors are familiar with taking out insurances for: All Risks; Public/Products Liability; Employers' Liability; Private/Commercial Motors; Professional Indemnity; and Other Ancillary Covers. Contractors should advise their insurance company or brokers that they are tendering under the new forms of Public Works Contract and provide the insurance company or broker with copies of the required Contract Insurances. There may be additional insurance premiums to meet the Contract requirements. These additional premiums will have to be included in the tender.
>
> It will be necessary for Contractors, when obtaining quotations from subcontractors, to provide the subcontractors with the Contract Insurance requirements, especially where there is a design element. Subcontractors can then incorporate the insurance requirements into their prices for inclusion in the tender. The situation is similar for subcontractors who do not have a design element.

E   Performance Bond
Sub-clause 1.5

A performance bond is/is not required. (*Delete one*. If none deleted, bond is required.)

The amount of the performance bond shall be ....% of the initial Contract Sum up to certification of Substantial Completion of the Works, and ....% of the initial Contract Sum for the subsequent period stated in the form of bond in the Works Requirements. (If not stated, 25% up to Substantial Completion, and 12.5% for 15 months after that.)

> **NOTE**
>
> Every contract is bondable. However, the level of risk undertaken by the Contractor determines the cost of the premium. It is recommended that that the bondsman is provided with a copy of the Contract, the Schedule and any specific requirements of the tender documents.
>
> Bid bonds may be required, especially where the Contract is subject to EU procurement rules. Bid bonds provide the Employer with a means of security in the event that the successful tenderer refuses to accept the Contract, as EU procurement rules do not allow the Contract to be awarded to the next unsuccessful tenderer. Bid bonds will be an exception rather than a rule. This again will attract a premium that will have to be included in the tender sum.

F   Collateral Warranties
Sub-clause 5.5

Collateral warranties are required from the following categories of Specialists, by the following dates; and the amount withheld from payments under sub-clause 11.4.1 are as follows:

Category of Specialist	Date for warranty	Amount withheld

> **NOTE**
>
> It is important at tender stage that all subcontractors, designers and professional service contracts (engineering, for example) are provided with a copy of the warranty required of them by the Employer. In the event that a successful tenderer does not provide the required warranties the Employer may withhold monies under clause 5 of the Contract.

G   Dates for Substantial Completion, Sections, liquidated damages, retention

(*Employer to complete names of sections*)	Date for Substantial Completion (*unless to be completed by Contractor in part 2*) (*Last day of period starting on the Contract Date or date*)	Rate of liquidated damages	Reduction in retention on Substantial Completion of Section (%)
The Works		€ ....per	
Section:		€ ....per	
Section:		€ ....per	
Section:		€ ....per	
Section:		€ ....per	

> **NOTE**
>
> These details will be provided by the Employer.

H   Early completion
Sub-clause 9.6

The Employer's Representative is/is not required to issue the certificate of Substantial Completion if the Works or a Section reaches Substantial Completion before its Date for Substantial Completion. (If neither deleted, read as 'is required'.)

> **NOTE**
>
> The Employer can exercise the option of not being obliged to issue a certificate of Substantial Completion in the event of the Contractor finishing early. In such an event, the Works remain the responsibility of the Contractor, to include security, insurances, and maintenance of mechanical and electrical components. The bond would not be released until Substantial Completion.

I   Defects Period

The initial Defects Period is .... from the date of Substantial Completion of the Works. (If none stated, one year.)

> **NOTE**
>
> The Employer will specify the Defects Period.

J   Random Checks for Employment Records

Sub-clause 5.3.3A(2) shall be/shall not be part of the Contract.
Delete as applicable. If neither is deleted, read as "shall be".

> **NOTE**
>
> The Employer can reserve the right to make random checks under sub-clause 5.3.3A(2) to establish that correct rates of pay apply to all operatives engaged on the project.

K   Delay Events, Compensation Events, Programme Contingency, Delay Costs, Adjustments
(Sub-clauses 9.3, 9.4, 10.1, 10.6, 10.7)

Delay Events and Compensation Events are as follows:
(*Employer to select "Yes" or "No" for compensation events 17–21. If any box is blank, read as "no".*)

Event	Delay Event	Compensation Event
1. The Employer's Representative gives the Contractor a Change Order	Yes	Yes
2. The Employer's Representative directs the Contractor to search for Defects or their cause and no Defect is found, and the search was not required because of a failure of the Contractor to comply with the Contract	Yes	Yes
3. The Employer's Representative directs the Contractor to suspend work under sub-clause 9.2	Yes	Yes
4. The Contractor suspends work in accordance with sub-clause 12.3	Yes	Yes
5. There is a factual error in information about the Site or setting out information in the Works Requirements. [This does not include an error of interpretation.]	Yes	Yes
6. The Employer takes over part of the Works before Substantial Completion of the Works and any relevant Section	Yes	Yes
7. The Employer's Representative does not give the Contractor an instruction required under sub-clause 4.5.4 within the time required under sub-clause 4.11.2 when the Contractor has asked for the instruction in accordance with sub-clause 4.11.1	Yes	Yes
8. The Employer does not allow the Contractor to occupy and use a part of the Site in accordance with sub-clause 7.1	Yes	Yes
9. The Employer does not give the Contractor a Works Item or other thing as required by the Contract when the Contractor has asked for it in accordance with sub-clause 4.11.1	Yes	Yes
10. Employer's Personnel working on the Site under clause 7.6 interfere with the execution of the Works on the Site, and the interference is unforeseeable and not in accordance with the Contract	Yes	Yes
11. The Employer instructs the Contractor under sub-clause 3.2.3 to rectify loss of or damage to Risk Items for which the Contractor is not responsible	Yes	Yes

Event		Delay Event	Compensation Event
12.	Loss of or damage to the Works that is at the Contractor's risk in accordance with sub-clause 3.2	Yes	No
13.	A **weather event as** described below	Yes	No
14.	A strike or lockout affecting the construction industry generally or a significant part of it, and not confined to employees of the Contractor or any Contractor's Personnel	Yes	No
15.	Delay to the Works caused by the order or other act of a court or other public authority exercising authority under Law, that did not arise as a result of or in connection with an act, omission or breach of Legal Requirements of the Contractor or the Contractor's Personnel or a breach of the Contract by the Contractor	Yes	No
16.	A breach by the Employer of the Contract delaying the Works that is not listed elsewhere in this table	Yes	Yes
17.	A difference between the Contract value of the Works according to the quantities and descriptions in a Bill of Quantities in the Pricing Document, if there is one, [taking into account the method of measurement and any amendments identified below] and the Contract value of the Works described in the Works Requirements, because the Bill of Quantities, when compared with the Works Requirements • includes an incorrect quantity or • includes an item that should not have been included or • excludes an item that should have been included or • gives an incorrect item description and the difference for an item in, or that should have been in, the Bill of Quantities is more than €500.	No	
18.	An item of archaeological interest or human remains is found on the Site, and it was unforeseeable	Yes	
19.	The Contractor encounters on the Site unforeseeable ground conditions or man-made obstructions in the ground, other than Utilities	Yes	
20.	The Contractor encounters unforeseeable Utilities in the ground on the Site	Yes	
21.	Owners of Utilities on the Site do not relocate or disconnect Utilities as stated in the Works Requirements, when the Contractor has complied with their procedures and the procedures in the Contract, and the failure is unforeseeable	Yes	

In the above table

> **Utilities** means conducting media and apparatus for water, sewage, electricity, gas, oil, telecommunications, data, steam, air, or other services, and associated apparatus and structures.

> A condition, circumstance or occurrence is **unforeseeable** if an experienced contractor tendering for the Works could not have reasonably foreseen it on the Designated Date, having inspected the Site and its surroundings and having satisfied itself, insofar as practicable and taking into account any

information in connection with the Site provided by the Employer, as to all matters concerning the Site, including its form and nature and its geotechnical, hydrological and climatic conditions.

If there is a Bill of Quantities, the **method of measurement** according to which it was prepared and measurements are to be made is .... except when any statement or general or detailed description of the work in the Contract shows the contrary.

A **weather event** is when for any month between the Starting Date and the Date for Substantial Completion of the Works, the value for any of the weather data listed below, as measured at .... weather station, is higher than the highest value occurring at least once every 10 years in the corresponding month of the year, on average according to historical data from the same station:

- cumulative rainfall for the month

- number of days in the month with rainfall exceeding 20mm

- number of days with minimum air temperature less than 0° Celsius

- number of days with maximum mean 10 minute wind speed exceeding 20 metres per second

- _____

If no weather station is named above, the Met Éireann weather station nearest the Site shall be used. If the weather station named above, or the nearest one, does not measure or record data for any of the above weather, the nearest station to the Site that measures and records that data shall be used for that weather.

In sub-clause 9.4:

- the **first threshold** is _____ Site Working Days of delay caused by Compensation Events

- the **second threshold** is _____ Site Working Days of delay caused by Compensation Events

The definition of craftspersons in part 2E (for sub-clause 10.6.4(1) includes the following additional categories:

_____

_____

In sub-clause 10.6.4(3), the rates to be used to determine the cost of plant are the rates in ....

modified as follows:

- rates will be considered in euro

- ....

and any rates in the Pricing Document.

In sub-clause 10.7, the amount to be added for delay cost is the daily rate tendered by the Contractor in the Schedule, part 2E (sub-clause 10.7.1(1))/the expenses unavoidably incurred as a result of the delay (sub-clause 10.7.1(2))

(*Delete as applicable.* If neither deleted, expenses unavoidably incurred as a result of the delay to be read as deleted.)

For purposes of sub-clause 10.7, the Contractor is to tender in part 2E a single daily rate for delay costs/ separate daily rates for delay costs for each of the following periods or parts of the Works:

- ○ _____

- ○ _____

- ○ _____

- ○ (If the above are blank, and sub-clause 10.7.1(1) applies, Contractor is to tender a single daily rate)

NOTE

Section K of Part 1 of the Schedule is where the Contractor will identify the risks transferred to the Contractor. Sub-clauses 9.3 (Delay and Extension of Time), 9.4 (Programme Contingency), 10.1 (Compensation Event), 10.6 (Adjustments to the Contract Sum) and 10.7 (Delay Cost) apply.

A Delay Event is when the Contractor becomes aware that work is being or is likely to be delayed. From the heading in the Contract, this will be at the heart of the Contract and will require the Contractor's attention.

There are 21 Delay Events and/or Compensation Events listed. Delay and Compensation Events are Items 1, 2, 3, 4, 5, 6, 7, 8, 9, 10, 11 and 16. Items 18, 19, 20 and 21 are Delay Events; however, compensation is electable by the Employer. Delay-only Events are items 12, 13, 14 and 15. The Compensation-only Event is Item 17, where compensation is electable by the Employer at tender stage. Taking each event in turn:

1 – *"The Employer's Representative gives the Contractor a Change Order"*. In Section A the limitations placed on the Employer's Representative will be specified. In the event that the Employer's Representative exceeds his powers the Contractor should query the instruction. It is thought at this stage that if the Employer's Representative exceeded his powers the Employer would be bound by the Employer's Representative instruction.

2 – *"The Employer's Representative directs the Contractor to search for defects or their cause and no defect is found… etc."* This can be both a Delay Event and a Compensation Event similar in terms to the GDLA clause 9 (Works to be Opened Up).

3 – *"The Employer's Representative directs the Contractor to suspend work under sub-clause 9.2 (Suspension)"*. This is both a Delay and Compensation Event.

4 – *"The Contractor suspends work in accordance with sub-clause 12.3 (Suspension by Contractor)"*. This is both a Delay and Compensation Event.

5 – *"There is a factual error in information about the Site or setting out information in the Works Requirements. [This does not include an error of interpretation.]"*. This is both a Delay and Compensation Event. An example of this would be incorrect ordinance survey datum or a part of the site not legally in the possession of the Employer.

6 – *"The Employer takes over part of the Works before Substantial Completion of the Works and any relevant Section"*. Should the Employer take over any part of the Works before the Contract Date for Substantial Completion, any resultant delays are Delay and Compensation Events. The Contractor has to consent to partial possession or sectional completion.

7 – *"The Employer's Representative does not give the Contractor an instruction required under sub-clause 4.5.4* [instructions] *within the time under sub-clause 4.11.2* [latest date for Employer's Representative to give required instructions] *when the Contractor has asked for instruction in accordance with sub-clause 4.11.1* [contractor to give at least 10 days' advance notice of the date the instruction is required]*"*. This is both a Delay and Compensation Event.

8 – *"The Employer does not allow the Contractor to occupy and use of a part of the Site in accordance with sub-clause 7.1* [Lands made available for the works]*"*. This is both a Delay and Compensation Event.

9 – *"The Employer does not give the Contractor a Works Item or other thing as required by the Contract when the Contractor has asked for it in accordance with sub-clause 4.11.1"*. This is identical to Item 7 above and is both a Delay and Compensation Event.

10 – *"Employer's Personnel working on the Site under clause 7.6 interfere with the execution of the Works on the Site, and the interference is unforeseeable and not in accordance with the Contract"*. This is both a Delay and Compensation Event. In the event that the interference is foreseeable then it is deemed to be included for within the Contractor's tender bid.

11 – *"The Employer instructs the Contractor under sub-clause 3.2.3* [Care Of The Works] *to rectify loss of or damage to Risk Items for which the Contractor is not responsible"*. This is both a Delay and Compensation Event.

The foregoing items are similar to variations occurring in the current standard forms.

The following items are Delay-only Events:

12 – *"Loss or damage to the Works that is at the Contractor's risk in accordance with sub-clause 3.2 [Care of the Works]"*. This is the alternative to Item 11 and is a Delay-only Event.

13 – *"A weather event as described below"*. This is a Delay-only Event. It is far more restricted than current standard forms and is defined against a parameter set out in the Contract which is a 10-year weather event. Rainfall, air temperature and wind speed are measured against records contained in the named weather station or, if a weather station is not named, then the nearest weather station shall be used.

14 – *"A strike or lockout affecting the construction industry generally or a significant part of it, and not confined to employees of the Contractor or any Contractor's Personnel"*. This is a Delay-only Event. Site-only strikes and lockouts are excluded.

15 – *"Delay to the Works caused by the order or other act of a court or other public authority exercising authority under Law, that did not arise as a result of or in connection with an act, omission or breach of Legal Requirements of the Contractor or the Contractor's Personnel or a breach of the Contract by the Contractor"*. This is a Delay-only Event. These are beyond either party's control, and are therefore delay only.

[End of delay only events.]

16 – *"A breach by the Employer of the Contract delaying the Works that is not listed elsewhere in this table"*. This is both a Delay and Compensation Event. This is a catch-all clause which empowers the Date for Substantial Completion to be adjusted for an item that is not already catered for in the Contract. This then prevents time becoming "at large".

17 – *"A difference between the Contract value of the Works according to the quantities and descriptions in a Bill of Quantities in the Pricing Document, if there is one, [taking into account the method of measurement and any amendments identified below] and the Contract value of the Works described in the Works Requirements, because the Bill of Quantities, when compared with the Works Requirements*

- *includes an incorrect quantity or*

- *includes an item that should not have been included or*

- *excludes an item that should have been included or*

- *gives an incorrect item description*

and the difference for an item in, or that should have been in, the Bill of Quantities is more than €500". This is not a Delay Event. Compensation at tender stage is client-electable (whether quantities form part of the Contract or not). Compensation items must exceed €500.

18 – *"An item of archaeological interest or human remains is found on the Site, and it was unforeseeable"*. An item of value or archaeological or geological interest or human remains being found on the site, which was unforeseeable, will be a Delay Event and compensation is electable. A discovery of these items has to be unforeseeable. So if there is evidence of the existence of such items in Employer's reports/surveys then they are foreseeable. Archaeological items exist in heritage towns, areas of historical interest and the like.

19 – *"The Contractor encounters on the Site unforeseeable ground conditions or man-made obstructions in the ground, other than Utilities"*. This may be a Delay Event and compensation is electable.

20 – *"The Contractor encounters unforeseeable Utilities in the ground on the site"*. This is a Delay Event and compensation is electable. Utilities means conducting media and apparatus for water, sewage, electricity, gas, oil, telecommunications, data, steam, air or other services and associated apparatus and structures.

21 – *"Owners of utilities on the Site do not relocate or disconnect Utilities as stated in with the Works Requirements, when the Contractor has complied with their procedures and the procedures in the Contract, and the failure is unforeseeable"*. This is a Delay Event and compensation is electable.

Sub-clause 9.4 [Programme Contingency] – *thresholds*. The Employer will state in the tender documents the number of days for the contingency for the first and second thresholds to be included within the Contractor's programme. The Contractor will have to include the cost related to the contingency for the first threshold within his tender. The threshold will be a number of Site Working Days' delay caused by Compensation Events for which the Contractor will not receive compensation. If the total number of Site Working Days' delay to Substantial Completion of the Works caused by Compensation Events (for which the Contractor would otherwise be entitled to an extension) is less than the first threshold, there shall be no extensions to the initial Date for Substantial Completion of the Works for delay caused by Compensation Events.

If the total number of Site Working Days' delay to Substantial Completion of the Works caused by Compensation Events (for which the Contractor would otherwise be entitled to an extension) exceeds the first threshold, there shall be deducted from the total number of Site Working Days' extension to the initial Date for Substantial Completion of the Works for delay caused by Compensation Events:

- the number of Site Working Days stated as the first threshold; and

- half the number of Site Working Days' delay to Substantial Completion of the Works caused by the Compensation Events (for which the Contractor would otherwise be entitled to an extension) after deducting the first threshold, but the total deduction under this paragraph (2) shall not exceed the second threshold.

If a successful tenderer includes contingency delay costs in his tender and the delays do not occur then the Contractor benefits.

L   Payment Particulars
Clause 11

Period for interim payment is .... (If none stated, monthly.)

Minimum amount for interim payments, except release of retention, €................ (If none stated, there is no minimum.)

When permitted by the Pricing Documents, up to _____% of the Contract value of unfixed Works Items may be included in an interim payment. (If none stated, 90%).

The retention percentage is ....%. (If none stated, 10%.)

> **NOTE**
>
> This section will specify the periods of payments. It will also specify the minimum amount for interim payments, the percentage of unfixed Works Items that will be paid and the retention percentage to apply.

M   Price Variation
Sub-clause 10.8

Clause PV1/Clause PV2 attached to this Schedule is part of the Contract. (Delete as applicable. If none deleted, Clause PV1 shall apply).

N   Conciliation and Arbitration
Sub-clause 13.1.2

Failing agreement, the conciliator will be appointed by ....

Sub-clause 13.2

The arbitration rules are the Public Works Arbitration Rules, 2007

The person or body to appoint the arbitrator, if not agreed by the parties, is

....

PART 2
(Completed by the Contractor and included with Tender)

A Communications
Sub-clause 4.14

The details for sending notices under clause 12 or 13 to the Contractor are
For the attention of ....
Address
....
....
....

The details for sending other notices to the Contractor are
For the attention of ....
Address
....
....
....
fax.......................................
email....................................

The Contractor's agent in the Republic of Ireland for service of legal process is
Name ....
Address
....
....
....
....

Note: An agent in the State must be named if the Contractor's registered office or other principal place of business is outside the State.

> **NOTE**
>
> The tenderer will provide details of the name and address of the individual within the company who will receive notices from the Employer under clauses 12 (Termination) and 13 (Conciliation and Arbitration). The tenderer will also provide details of names and addresses for the Employer to serve other notices.

B Parent Company Guarantee
Sub-clause 1.6

The Contractor shall provide a parent company guarantee in the form in the Works Requirements from
....
(*name and address of parent company, registered address and place where incorporated or organised*). If none named, no parent company guarantee required.

Note: Tenderers must name a guarantor if parent company has been identified for purposes of suitability assessment.

C   Works Proposals

The **Works Proposals** are

....
....
....
....
....
....

> **NOTE**
>
> The tenderer shall list these documents that comprise the Works Proposals and these will reflect the Works Requirements as requested by the Employer.

D   Dates for Substantial Completion

	Date for Substantial Completion: Number of days after the Contract Date *(to be completed by Contractor in Tender* **ONLY** *if not completed by Employer in Part 1)*
The Works	
Section: *(Employer to complete name of Section)*	
Section: *(Employer to complete name of Section)*	
Section: *(Employer to complete name of Section)*	
Section: *(Employer to complete name of Section)*	

> **NOTE**
>
> The tenderer shall complete the dates for Substantial Completion if not completed by the Employer in Part 1.

E   Adjustments to the Contract Sum including Delay Costs
Sub-clauses 10.6 *and* 10.7

The Contractor's tendered hourly rates for labour and related costs [including PRSI, benefits, tool money, travelling time and country money]:

- Craftspersons   € ....per hour

- General Operatives €............per hour

- Apprentices   €............per hour

(If left blank, or stated as a negative value, read as zero.)

Craftspersons means those categories of work persons described as "craftsmen" or "electricians" in employment agreements registered under the Industrial Relations Acts 1946 to 2004, and, any additional categories listed in part 1K.

General Operatives means all direct labour other than craftspersons and apprentices.

Apprentices means categories of work persons under a contract of apprenticeship for trades whose practitioners fall within the above definition of craftspersons.

The Contractor's tendered percentage addition for costs of materials.................%

The Contractor's tendered percentage addition/deduction for costs of plant...................%

All of the above shall include on-costs, overheads and profit, and exclude VAT.
(If either of the above is left blank, read as zero.)

The Contractor's tendered rate of delay costs is €................. excluding VAT per Site Working Day. (If left blank, or stated as a negative value, read as zero.)

If part 1K states that separate rates are to be tendered for separate periods or parts of the Works, the Contractor's tendered rates are as follows:

Period or part of the Works (part 1K)	Tendered Rate
○	€...........................per Site Working Day
○	€...........................per Site Working Day
○	€...........................per Site Working Day

---

NOTE

This section will be the most difficult and challenging for Contractors and will play a key role in determining the success of the tender bid.

All-in hourly rates for craftspersons, general operatives and apprentices will have to be completed. There are no differentiations in the categories of craftspersons or the grades of apprentices. A number of delay hours for operatives will be provided by the Employer.

A percentage addition to the cost of materials will have to be quoted.

A percentage addition to the cost of plant will have to be quoted.

Sub-clause 10.7 of the Schedule requires the Contractor to state the amount per day he will be recompensed for site delays. The figures will also be used by the Employer to establish the most economically advantageous tender.

The Contractor will have to calculate a site daily delay cost which will include his own costs, in addition to sub-contactors' and all other costs. There is no scope for recovering any further additional costs.

The daily amount quoted by the Contractor in the Schedule Part 2E is the amount by which the Contract Sum will be adjusted for delays arising from Delay and Compensation Events only, regardless of whether or not the Contractor's full costs are covered.

In the event that a Contractor leaves the site daily delay cost blank then the amount is taken as zero.

The Employer may request site daily delay costs for different periods or portions of the Works. The Contractor has to quote these rates within his tender.

Most Economically Advantageous Tender

In assessing the tenders, to achieve the most economically advantageous tender, the Employer will add to the tendered sum for the Works the following figures that the Contractor has to quote in his tender:

(i) The delay days multiplied by the tendered site daily cost;
(ii) The hours for works persons multiplied by the tendered hourly rates;
(iii) The tendered percentage addition for materials;
(iv) The tendered percentage addition for plant.

PUBLIC WORKS CONTRACTS

MODEL FORMS

CONTENTS

Text in gray italics identifies items to be filled-in by the Employer when these forms are included in Works Requirements.

MODEL FORM 1

FORM OF TENDER

[*Date*]

To [*Name and address of Employer*]
For the attention of [*contact person identified in tender documents*]

[*Name of Contract*]

A Dhaoine Uaisle

We have examined and understand the [*insert full name of selected contract form*], the Works Requirements, the Pricing Document, [Novated Design Documents] all as amended by any supplemental information, for the above contract. Terms used in this Tender that are defined in those documents have the same meaning in this Tender. We submit with this Tender the completed Pricing Document and Schedule [and Works Proposals listed in the attached Schedule Part 2], which form part of this Tender. [We adopt the Novated Design Documents as our Works Proposals].

We offer to complete the Works on the terms of and in conformity with the documents referred to in the preceding paragraph for the lump sum of ....
.... euro including VAT, as adjusted in accordance with the Contract.

In preparing this Tender we have taken account of the obligations relating to employment protection and working conditions that are in force in the place where the works are to be carried out, including the Contract requirements.

We agree that this offer will remain open for your acceptance at any time until the latest of:

- the end of the period specified in your invitation to tender

- expiry of at least 21 days written notice to terminate this Tender given by us.

Your acceptance of this Tender within that time will result in the Contract being formed between us.

We agree that you are not bound to accept the lowest or any tender you may receive.

Is sinne, le meas

Given under the tenderer's common seal

....

....
(*signatures of persons authorised to authenticate the seal*)

affix common seal

OR Signed, sealed and delivered by
.... (*name of attorney*)
as lawful attorney of the tenderer
under a power of attorney dated ....

in the presence of
....(*signature of witness*)
....(*name of witness*)
....(*witness' occupation*)
....(*witness' address*)

....
(*signature of attorney*)
affix attorney's personal seal

OR (*if the tenderer is an individual*)
Signed, sealed and delivered by

....(*name of tenderer*)

in the presence of

....(*signature of witness*)
....(*name of witness*)
....(*witness' occupation*)
....(*witness' address*)

....
(*signature of tenderer*)
affix Contractor's personal seal

Note: If the tenderer is a partnership or joint venture, execution must be by each member, using the blocks below.

Joint venture member 1

Given under the common seal of

.... (*name of joint venture member 1*)

....

....
(*signatures of persons authorised to authenticate the seal*)

affix common seal

OR **Signed, sealed and delivered** by

.... (*name of attorney*)

as lawful attorney of ....
(*name of joint venture member 1*)

under a power of attorney dated ....

in the presence of

....(*signature of witness*)
....(*name of witness*)
....(*witness' occupation*)
....(*witness' address*)

....
(*signature of attorney*)
affix attorney's personal seal

Joint venture member 2

Given under the common seal of

.... (*name of joint venture member 2*)

....

....
(*signatures of persons authorised to authenticate the seal*)

affix common seal

OR **Signed, sealed and delivered** by

.... (*name of attorney*)

as lawful attorney of ....
(*name of joint venture member 2*)

under a power of attorney dated ....

in the presence of

....(*signature of witness*)
....(*name of witness*)
....(*witness' occupation*)
....(*witness' address*)

....
(*signature of attorney*)
affix attorney's personal seal

Joint venture member 3

Given under the common seal of

.... (*name of joint venture member 3*)   affix common seal

....

....

(*signatures of persons authorised to authenticate the seal*)

OR **Signed, sealed and delivered** by

.... (*name of attorney*)

as lawful attorney of ....

(*name of joint venture member 3*)

under a power of attorney dated ....

in the presence of   (*signature of attorney*)

affix attorney's personal seal

....(*signature of witness*)

....(*name of witness*)

....(*witness' occupation*)

....(*witness' address*)

[SCHEDULE TO BE APPENDED –

PART 1 TO BE COMPLETED BY EMPLOYER IN ISSUED DOCUMENTS

PART 2 TO BE COMPLETED BY TENDERER AND SUBMITTED WITH TENDER]

MODEL FORM 2

FORM OF BID BOND

[*Date*]

TO [*Name and address of Employer*]

[*Name of Contract*]

[*Name and address of bidder*] (the **Bidder**) proposes to submit a tender to you for the above contract. It is a requirement for submitting the tender that a bond, in these terms and in the amount of [10]% of the amount of the tendered contract sum, be submitted with the tender.

BY THIS BID BOND, we, ... [*Name and address of Surety*] guarantee to you that, if you accept the bidder's tender, the bidder will, within the time required by the contract formed by that acceptance, execute under seal and deliver the Agreement referred to in that contract and give you the fully executed and delivered performance bond and other documents required under clause 9.1 of the Conditions of that contract, all in compliance with the contract. If the bidder fails to do so, or otherwise repudiates its tender, we will, subject to this bond, pay all the loss you sustain as a result, up to the maximum of €...

This bond will expire on [[120] days after the last date for receipt of tender], when we will be released of liability under it, unless you have before that date notified us that the bidder has defaulted in any of the obligations guaranteed by this bond.

We will not be released in any way or discharged by time, indulgence, waiver, alteration, release or compromise or any other circumstances that might operate as a release of a guarantor at law or in equity.

This bond is governed by and construed according to Irish law and we submit to the jurisdiction of the Irish courts to determine all matters concerning it.

We appoint .... of .... as our agent for the service of legal proceedings. We confirm that the named agent has been irrevocably appointed and the agent's failure to notify us of receipt of a document will not invalidate any proceedings or the service of the document.[1]

Given under our common seal

---

[1] An address in Ireland is required when the Surety does not have a registered office in Ireland.

MODEL FORM 3

FORM OF LETTER TO APPARENTLY UNSUCCESSFUL TENDERERS

[*Date*]

To [*Name and address of unsuccessful tenderer*]

[*Name of Contract*]

A Dhaoine Uaisle

I write to inform you that we have assessed the tenders received for the above contract and have determined that the most economically advantageous tender was submitted by ....

It is our intention [subject to the approval of [*funding department*]] to enter into the contract with that tenderer. It is anticipated that a letter of acceptance will issue to them not earlier than [14] days from the date of this letter.

I would like to thank you for the interest you have shown in this competition.

Please acknowledge receipt of this letter.

Is mise, le meas

Signed: ....
On behalf of the Employer

MODEL FORM 4

FORM OF LETTER OF INTENT

[*Date*]

To [*Name and address of bidder*]

[*Name of Contract*]

Subject to Contract/Contract Denied

A Dhaoine Uaisle

I refer to your tender for the above contract.

I write to inform you that we intend to issue a Letter of Acceptance to you within 14 days after receiving the following items:

- Performance Bond in the form included in the Works Requirements
- evidence of the insurances required by the contract
- Tax Clearance Certificate
- [*add any other conditions, e.g. funding approval, manager's order, board approval, parent company guarantee, collateral warranties*]

If any of the above listed items are not provided within [•] days of the date of this letter, we may proceed to award the Contract to another tenderer.

This is not the Letter of Acceptance. The Employer has not accepted your tender.

Please return a copy of this letter acknowledging receipt as indicated below.

Is mise, le meas

Signed: ....
On behalf of the Employer

We acknowledge receipt of this letter on ....

Signed: ....
On behalf of the Contractor

MODEL FORM 5

FORM OF LETTER OF ACCEPTANCE

[*Date*]

To [*Name and address of Contractor*]

[*Name of Contract*]

A Dhaoine Uaisle

I refer to your tender for the above Contract dated .... (the **Tender**). Terms used in this letter that are defined in the Conditions of that Contract have the same meaning in this letter.

I write to inform you that [*name of Employer*] accepts the Tender. This is the Letter of Acceptance referred to in the Conditions.

The contract formed by this acceptance consists of the following documents:

- This Letter of Acceptance

- The Agreement

- The Conditions of [*insert full name of the selected form of public works contract*]

- The Schedule appended to this Letter of Acceptance

- The Works Requirements identified in the Schedule

- The Pricing Documents identified in the Schedule

- The Works Proposals identified in the Schedule (including any Novated Design Documents identified in the Schedule)

- The following post-tender clarifications:

    ....
    ....
    ....
    ....

The Contract Sum is ....euro, including VAT.

I draw attention to your obligations in clause 9.1 of the conditions about documents to be provided before the Starting Date.

Please return to me a copy of this letter acknowledging receipt as indicated below.

Is mise, le meas

Signed: ....
On behalf of the Employer
Duly authorised to accept the Tender

We acknowledge receipt of this letter on ....

Signed: ....
On behalf of the Contractor

SCHEDULE TO BE APPENDED

MODEL FORM 6

FORM OF PERFORMANCE BOND
(Clause 1.5)

Bond No...............................
BOND AMOUNT: €...

THIS BOND is made on ....

BETWEEN

1.   ....,
     whose registered office is at .... (the **Contractor**)

2.   ....,
     whose registered office is at .... (the **Surety**) and

3.   [*name of Employer*] (the **Employer**)

BACKGROUND

A.   By a contract (the **Contract**), the Contractor has been or will be appointed by the Employer for [*name of Contract*]

B.   The Contractor has agreed to furnish a performance bond to the Employer.

C.   Terms defined in the Contract have the same meaning in this Bond.

IT IS AGREED AS FOLLOWS:

1.   The Surety guarantees to the Employer that if the Contractor breaches the Contract or the Contractor's obligation to complete the Works is terminated under clause 12.1 of the Conditions the Surety will, subject to this Bond, pay all amounts for which the Contractor is liable under or as damages for breach of the Contract, as established under the Contract, taking into account all sums due to the Contractor under the Contract.

2.   The maximum liability of the Surety under this Bond will not exceed €................................... This amount will be reduced by half on issue of the certificate of Substantial Completion of the Works under the Contract.

3.   No alteration in the Contract or in the extent or nature of the works to be done under it, and no allowance of time under the Contract, and no forbearance or forgiveness concerning the Contract by the Employer, will in any way release the Surety from liability under this Bond.

4.   The Surety will be released from its liability under this Bond [•] days after the certificate of Substantial Completion of the Works has been issued, except in relation to any breach by the Contractor or termination that has occurred before that date, written notice (including particulars of the breach or termination) of which has been given to the Surety earlier than 4 weeks after this expiry date.

5.   The Contractor undertakes to the Surety to perform its obligations under the Contract. This undertaking does not limit any rights or remedies of the Employer or the Surety.

6.   The Contractor must promptly, and the Employer may, provide to the Surety by registered or hand-delivered letter to the Surety's registered office given above or to the agent named in clause 12 below a copy of any notice that the Contractor gives to or receives from the Employer under clause 12 of the Conditions. Breach by the Contractor of this obligation or failure to give notice will not give any defence to a call on this Bond.

7.   The decision of a court or arbitrator in a dispute between the Employer and the Contractor will be binding on the Surety as to all matters concerning a breach of the Contract, termination under the Contract, and the Contractor's liability.

8. If the Surety is called on to pay the Employer's loss following a termination under clause 12.1 of the Conditions, the Surety may suggest a completion contractor to the Employer, but the Employer has no obligation to accept the suggestion.

9. The Surety will not be liable under this Bond for a breach or termination caused solely and directly by war, invasion, act of foreign enemies, hostilities (whether war is declared or not), civil war, rebellion, revolution, or military or usurped power.

10. The Employer may assign the benefit of this Bond, without the Surety's or the Contractor's consent, by giving written notice to the Surety.

11. This Bond is governed by and construed according to Irish law and the parties submit to the jurisdiction of the Irish courts to determine all matters concerning it.

12. [The Surety appoints .... of .... as its agent for service of legal proceedings. The Surety confirms that the named agent has been irrevocably appointed and the failure of the agent to notify the Surety of receipt of a document will not invalidate any proceedings or the service of the document.][2]

13. Money payable by the Surety under this Bond will be paid in euro in Ireland.

Given under the Contractor's common seal

Given under the Surety's common seal

Signed on behalf of the Employer

....

in the presence of

....

---

[2] An address in Ireland is required when the Surety does not have a registered office in Ireland.

MODEL FORM 7

FORM OF PARENT COMPANY GUARANTEE
(Clause 1.6)

THIS GUARANTEE is made on ....

BETWEEN

1.   ....,
      whose registered office is at .... (the **Contractor**)

2.   ....,
      whose registered office is at ....(the **Guarantor**) and

3.   [*name of Employer*] whose principal office is at [*insert*] (the **Employer**)

BACKGROUND

A   By a Contract (the **Contract**) the Contractor has been or will be appointed by the Employer for [*name of Contract*]

B   The Guarantor has agreed to guarantee the Contractor's performance of the Contract.

IT IS AGREED AS FOLLOWS:

1.   **Guarantee**

      The Guarantor irrevocably and unconditionally:

      1.1   guarantees to the Employer that the Contractor will punctually perform all its obligations under the Contract and

      1.2   undertakes to the Employer to fully perform the Contractor's obligations under the Contract if the Contractor fails to perform them.

2.   **Indemnity**

      If the Contractor's obligations under the Contract are or become void or unenforceable then, as between the Guarantor and the Employer (but without affecting the Contractor's obligations), the Guarantor will as principal obligor indemnify the Employer against any resulting loss and be liable to the Employer for the same amount as the Guarantor would have been liable for if the obligations had not been void or unenforceable.

3.   **Contractor's failure to perform**

      3.1   If the Contractor goes into liquidation, administration, examinership or receivership or becomes subject to any other form of insolvency proceedings, or if the Contractor's obligation to complete the Works is lawfully terminated under sub-clause 12.1 of the Conditions of the Contract, any such event will be conclusive evidence, for the purposes of this Guarantee, that the Contractor has failed to perform the Contract.

      3.2   The decision of a court or arbitrator or an agreement between the Contractor and the Employer will be binding on the Guarantor in relation to any failure by the Contractor to perform the Contract.

4.   **Guarantee is in addition to other security**

      The Guarantor's obligations are in addition to and independent of any other security the Employer may at any time hold for the Contractor's obligations under the Contract.

5. **Continuing guarantee**

The Guarantor's liability will continue until the Contractor has performed all its obligations in full, and will not be satisfied or diminished by any payment or recovery of an amount due from the Contractor to the Employer.

6. **Guarantor's liability not impaired**

The Guarantor's liability under this Guarantee is as principal obligor and not merely as surety. Neither the Guarantor's liability under this Guarantee nor the Employer's rights under it will be affected by any of the following, whether or not known to any of the parties:

6.1. the Contractor's obligations under the Contract being or becoming illegal, invalid or unenforceable, if it would not be illegal for the Guarantor to fulfil the obligation

6.2. bankruptcy, insolvency, liquidation, examinership, dissolution, amalgamation, winding up, reorganisation or any similar proceeding concerning the Contractor

6.3. change in the status, function, control or ownership of the Contractor

6.4. death or incapacity of the Contractor

6.5. amendment to the Contract or change to the works to be done under it (whether or not the amendment or change increases the Guarantor's liability)

6.6. time being given to the Contractor

6.7. a concession, arrangement, waiver or other indulgence being granted or made or agreed to be granted or made by the Employer

6.8. anything that the Employer or the Contractor do or fail to do, including without limitation:

(1) asserting or pursuing (or failing or delaying to assert, perfect or enforce) rights or remedies or

(2) giving security or releasing, modifying, or exchanging security or

(3) having or incurring any liability

6.9. assignment of the benefit of the Contract

6.10. whole or partial discharge (whether of the Contractor's obligations or security for them or otherwise) or arrangement made on the faith of payment, security or other disposition that is avoided or must be repaid on bankruptcy, liquidation or otherwise

6.11. rights against third parties that the Employer may have relating to performance of the Contractor's obligations

6.12. a reduction in, or other arrangement relating to, the Contractor's liability to the Employer as a result of an arrangement or composition under the Companies (Amendment) Act, 1990 or any similar provision

6.13. any other act, event, fact, circumstance, rule of law, or omission.

7. **Guarantor not to claim against or in competition with the Employer**

For as long as the Contractor has actual or contingent obligations or liability under the Contract, the Guarantor shall not:

7.1. be entitled to share in the Employer's rights under the Contract or any other rights or security of the Employer or

7.2. in competition with the Employer, seek to enforce any rights concerning the Guarantor performing or having obligations under this Guarantee

and if the Guarantor receives money from the Contractor in relation to a payment of the Guarantor under this Guarantee, the Guarantor will hold the money in trust for the Employer as long as the Guarantor has any liability (contingent or otherwise) under this Guarantee.

8. **No preconditions upon Employer**

The Employer may enforce this Guarantee without exercising rights against the Contractor or anyone else.

9. **Assignment**

The Employer may assign the benefit of this Guarantee without the Guarantor's or Contractor's consent. The Employer shall give notice to the Guarantor within 28 days after any assignment.

10. **Partial invalidity**

If at any time any part of this Guarantee is or becomes illegal, invalid or unenforceable, the rest of this Guarantee will remain legal, valid and enforceable.

11. **Law and Jurisdiction**

This Guarantee is governed by and construed according to Irish law and the parties submit to the jurisdiction of the Irish courts to determine all matters concerning it.

12. **Notices**

Any communication given in connection with this Guarantee must be in writing and delivered to, or sent by pre-paid registered post to the relevant party's address at the top of this Guarantee, or the Guarantor's agent's address in clause 13 below, or another address notified in writing by the relevant party. Pre-paid registered post is taken to have been received 2 days after it was sent.

13. **Agent for Service**

[The Guarantor appoints .... of ....
as its agent for service of legal proceedings. The Guarantor confirms that the named agent has been irrevocably appointed and the failure of the agent to notify the Guarantor of receipt of a document will not invalidate any proceedings or the service of the document.][3]

14. **Representations and Warranties**

The Guarantor represents and warrants to the Employer that:

14.1. the execution, delivery and performance of this Guarantee by the Guarantor has been duly and validly authorised by all requisite corporate action by the Guarantor and

14.2. this Guarantee is the Guarantor's legal, valid and binding obligation in accordance with its terms and

14.3. no approval or consent from any governmental entity or any other person or entity is required in connection with the execution, delivery or performance of this Guarantee by the Guarantor.

Given under the Guarantor's comm on seal

....
....

---

[3] An address in Ireland is required when the Guarantor does not have a registered office in Ireland.

Given under the Contractor's common seal

....

....

Signed on behalf of the Employer

....

in the presence of

....

MODEL FORM 8

FORM OF NOVATION AND GUARANTEE DEED
(To be used when the Contract is to be novated to a joint venture company)

THIS DEED is made on ....

BETWEEN

1. ....,
   whose registered office is at .... (the **Contractor**)

2. ....,
   whose registered office is at ....

   ....,
   whose registered office is at ....

   ....,
   whose registered office is at ....

   (together, the **Guarantors**) and

3. [*name of Employer*] whose principal office is at [*insert*] (the **Employer**)

BACKGROUND

A. By a Contract (the **Contract**) the Guarantors have been appointed by the Employer for [*name of Contract*]

B. The Guarantors have formed the Contractor as their subsidiary for the purpose of completing the Contract.

C. This deed is for the Contract to be novated from the Employer and the Guarantors to the Employer and the Contractor, and for the Guarantor jointly and severally to guarantee the Contractor's performance of the Contract.

IT IS AGREED AS FOLLOWS:

1. **No amount due**

    The Guarantors acknowledge that no amount is due to them under the Contract on the date of this Deed.

2. **Novation**

    The Contract is novated from the Employer of the one part and the Guarantors of the other to the Employer of the one part and the Contractor of the other.

3. **Contract affirmed**

    3.1. Subject to this Deed, the Contract remains in effect.

    3.2. The Contractor is bound and treated as if always bound to perform the Contractor's obligations and observe the Contract as if the Contractor were and always had been named as "the Contractor" in the Contract in place of the Guarantors.

    3.3. The Employer is bound and treated as if always bound to perform the Employer's obligations and observe the Contract for the benefit of the Contractor as if the Contractor were and always had been named as "the Contractor" in the Contract in place of the Guarantors.

4. **Warranty**

The Guarantors and the Contractor represent and warrant to the Employer that the Contractor's duties and obligations under the Contract have been performed in accordance with the Contract.

5. **Guarantee**

The Guarantors irrevocably and unconditionally:

5.1.   guarantee to the Employer that the Contractor will punctually perform all its obligations under the Contract and

5.2.   undertake to the Employer to fully perform the Contractor's obligations under the Contract if the Contractor fails to perform them.

6. **Indemnity**

If the Contractor's obligations under the Contract are or become void or unenforceable then, as between the Guarantor and the Employer (but without affecting the Contractor's obligations), the Guarantor will as principal obligor indemnify the Employer against any resulting loss and be liable to the Employer for the same amount as the Guarantor would have been liable for if the obligations had not been void or unenforceable.

7. **Contractor's failure to perform**

7.1.   If the Contractor goes into liquidation, administration, examinership or receivership or becomes subject to any other form of insolvency proceedings, or if the Contractor's obligation to complete the Works is lawfully terminated under sub-clause 12.1 of the Conditions of the Contract, any such event will be conclusive evidence, for the purposes of this Deed, that the Contractor has failed to perform the Contract.

7.2.   The decision of a court or arbitrator or an agreement between the Contractor and the Employer will be binding on the Guarantors in relation to any failure by the Contractor to perform the Contract.

8. **Guarantee is in addition to other security**

The Guarantors' obligations are in addition to and independent of any other security the Employer may at any time hold for the Contractor's obligations under the Contract.

9. **Continuing guarantee**

The Guarantors' liability will continue until the Contractor has performed all its obligations in full, and will not be satisfied or diminished by any payment or recovery of an amount due from the Contractor to the Employer.

10. **Joint and several liability**

The Guarantors' liability under this Deed is joint and several.

11. **Guarantor's liability not impaired**

The Guarantor's liability under this Guarantee is as principal obligor and not merely as surety. Neither the Guarantors' liability under this Deed nor the Employer's rights under it will be affected by any of the following, whether or not known to any of the parties:

11.1.   the Contractor's obligations under the Contract being or becoming illegal, invalid or unenforceable, if it would not be illegal for the Guarantor to fulfil the obligation

11.2.   bankruptcy, insolvency, liquidation, examinership, dissolution, amalgamation, winding up, reorganisation or any similar proceeding concerning the Contractor

11.3.   change in the status, function, control or ownership of the Contractor

11.4.   death or incapacity of the Contractor

11.5.   amendment to the Contract or change to the works to be done under it (whether or not the amendment or change increases the Guarantors' liability)

11.6.   time being given to the Contractor

11.7.   a concession, arrangement, waiver or other indulgence being granted or made or agreed to be granted or made by the Employer

11.8.   anything that the Employer or the Contractor do or fail to do, including without limitation:

(1)   asserting or pursuing (or failing or delaying to assert, perfect or enforce) rights or remedies or

(2)   giving security or releasing, modifying, or exchanging security or

(3)   having or incurring any liability

11.9.   assignment of the benefit of the Contract

11.10. whole or partial discharge (whether of the Contractor's obligations or security for them or otherwise) or arrangement made on the faith of payment, security or other disposition that is avoided or must be repaid on bankruptcy, liquidation or otherwise

11.11. rights against third parties that the Employer may have relating to performance of the Contractor's obligations

11.12. a reduction in, or other arrangement relating to, the Contractor's liability to the Employer as a result of an arrangement or composition under the Companies (Amendment) Act, 1990 or any similar provision

11.13. any other act, event, fact, circumstance, rule of law, or omission.

12. Guarantors not to claim against or in competition with the Employer

For as long as the Contractor has actual or contingent obligations or liability under the Contract, the Guarantors shall not:

12.1.   be entitled to share in the Employer's rights under the Contract or any other rights or security of the Employer or

12.2.   in competition with the Employer, seek to enforce any rights concerning the Guarantor performing or having obligations under this Deed

and if a Guarantor receives money from the Contractor in relation to a payment of the Guarantor under this Guarantee, the Guarantor will hold the money in trust for the Employer as long as the Guarantor has any liability (contingent or otherwise) under this Guarantee.

13. No preconditions upon Employer

The Employer may enforce this Deed without exercising rights against the Contractor or anyone else.

14. Assignment

The Employer may assign the benefit of this Guarantee without the Guarantors' or Contractor's consent. The Employer shall give notice to the Guarantor within 28 days after any assignment.

15. Partial invalidity

If at any time any part of this Deed is or becomes illegal, invalid or unenforceable, the rest of this Guarantee will remain legal, valid and enforceable.

16. Law and Jurisdiction

This Deed is governed by and construed according to Irish law and the parties submit to the jurisdiction of the Irish courts to determine all matters concerning it.

17. **Notices**

Any communication given in connection with this Deed must be in writing and delivered to, or sent by pre-paid registered post to the relevant party's address at the top of this Guarantee, or a Guarantor's agent's address in clause 18 below, or another address notified in writing by the relevant party. Pre-paid registered post is taken to have been received 2 days after it was sent.

18. **Agent for Service**

[The Guarantors appoint .... of .... as its agent for service of legal proceedings. The Guarantors confirm that the named agent has been irrevocably appointed and the failure of the agent to notify the Guarantor of receipt of a document will not invalidate any proceedings or the service of the document.][4]

19. **Representations and Warranties**

The Guarantors and the Contractor represent and warrant to the Employer that:

19.1.   The Guarantors own the entire beneficial interest in the share capital and issued share capital of the Contractor and no-one else is entitled to appoint members of the Contractor's board of directors or to vote at meetings of the members of the Contractor.

19.2.   the execution, delivery and performance of this Guarantee by the Guarantors and the Contractor has been duly and validly authorised by all requisite corporate action by the Guarantors and the Contractor and

19.3.   this Deed is the Guarantors' and the Contractor's legal, valid and binding obligation in accordance with its terms and

19.4.   no approval or consent from any governmental entity or any other person or entity is required in connection with the execution, delivery or performance of this Deed by the Guarantors or the Contractor.

Given under the Guarantors' common seals

....

....

....

....

....

Given under the Contractor's common seal

....

....

Signed on behalf of the Employer

....

in the presence of

....

---

4 An address in Ireland is required when the Surety does not have a registered office in Ireland.

MODEL FORM 9

FORM OF APPOINTMENT OF PROJECT SUPERVISOR FOR CONSTRUCTION STAGE ONLY

THIS DEED is made on ....

BETWEEN

1. .... (the **Client**) and

2. ....
   whose registered office is at .... (the **Project Supervisor**)

BACKGROUND

A. By a contract (the **Contract**) made on or about (date of letter of acceptance) the Client, as employer, has appointed [the Project Supervisor or ....] as contractor (the **Contractor**), for [*name of Contract*] (the **Works**).

B. This Deed is collateral to the Contract.

IT IS AGREED AS FOLLOWS:

1. The Client appoints the Project Supervisor as project supervisor for the construction stage according to the Safety, Health and Welfare (Construction) Regulations 2006, and any amendment to them (the Construction Regulations) for the project comprising the Works [and – *specify any additional scope for which this Project Supervisor is to be appointed project supervisor for construction stage, for example a process installation*] (the **Project**).

2. The Project Supervisor's appointment starts on the date of this Deed and continues for as long as, under the Construction Regulations, the Client is required to have a project supervisor for the construction stage for the Project, unless the appointment is terminated earlier.

3. The Project Supervisor accepts the appointment.

4. The Project Supervisor shall perform all of its duties under the Construction Regulations as project supervisor for the construction stage for the Project.

5. The Project Supervisor represents and warrants to the Client that the Project Supervisor is and will continue to be a competent person to carry out its duties under this Deed and the Construction Regulations and has allocated and will allocate sufficient resources to enable itself to comply with the requirements and prohibitions imposed on the Project Supervisor by this Deed and under the relevant statutory provisions. In this Deed, **competent person** and **relevant statutory provisions** are construed according to section 2 of the Safety, Health and Welfare at Work Act 2005, and any amendment to it.

6. The Project Supervisor represents and warrants to the Client that the time allowed by the Contract for the completion of the Works is appropriate and sufficient to enable the Project Supervisor to perform its duties under this Deed and the Construction Regulations.

7. The Project Supervisor represents and warrants to the Client that the information provided by the Client to the Project Supervisor about the state or condition of the Site (as defined in the Contract) and any premises on it is appropriate and sufficient to enable the Project Supervisor to perform its duties under this Deed and the Construction Regulations.

8. The Project Supervisor shall ensure that it is insured by insurances in the same terms as the insurances the Contractor is required to have under clauses 3.6 and 3.7 of the Conditions of the Contract, and that those insurances comply with all the requirements of the Contract, and are kept in force for the same period as required by the Contract, and include cover for death or injury resulting from the Project Supervisor's performance or non-performance of its duties under this Deed and the Construction Regulations.

9.   If the Project Supervisor breaches its obligations or warranties under this Deed, or if the Contractor's obligation to complete the Works is terminated under the Contract, the Client may terminate the Project Supervisor's appointment under this Deed.

10. Without limiting its obligations under the Construction Regulations, the Project Supervisor shall give the Client all documents it prepares in the course of and for the purpose of performing its duties under this Deed (**Project Supervisor's Documents**). If the Project Supervisor's appointment under this Deed terminates, the Project Supervisor shall give all Project Supervisor's Documents to the Client immediately. Ownership of and copyright in the Project Supervisor's Documents shall become the Client's when the Project Supervisor delivers them to the Client, or the appointment is terminated, whichever is earlier. The Project Supervisor shall indemnify the Client against any liability resulting from the use or copying of the Project Supervisor's Documents infringing the property (including intellectual property) rights of any person.

11. This Deed is governed by and construed according to Irish law. The parties submit to the jurisdiction of the Irish courts in relation to all matters concerning it.

Given under the Client's seal

Given under the Project Supervisor's common seal

MODEL FORM 10

FORM OF APPOINTMENT OF PROJECT SUPERVISOR FOR CONSTRUCTION STAGE AND DESIGN PROCESS

THIS DEED is made on ....

BETWEEN

1. .... (the **Client**) and

2. ....
   whose registered office is at .... (the **Project Supervisor**)

BACKGROUND

By a contract (the Contract) made on or about (date of letter of acceptance), the Client, as employer, has appointed [the Project Supervisor or ....] as contractor (the **Contractor**), for [*insert name of Contract*] (the **Works**).

This Deed is collateral to the Contract.

IT IS AGREED AS FOLLOWS:

1. The Client appoints the Project Supervisor as project supervisor for the design process and the construction stage according to the Safety, Health and Welfare (Construction) Regulations 2006, and any amendment to them (the **Construction Regulations**) for the project comprising the Works [and – *specify any additional scope for which this Project Supervisor is to be appointed project supervisor for construction stage, for example a process installation*] (the **Project**).

2. The Project Supervisor's appointment starts on the date of this Deed and continues for as long as, under the Construction Regulations, the Client is required to have a project supervisor for the design process or the construction stage for the Project, unless the appointment is terminated earlier.

3. The Project Supervisor accepts the appointment.

4. The Project Supervisor shall perform all of its duties under the Construction Regulations as project supervisor for the design process and construction stage for the Project.

5. The Project Supervisor represents and warrants to the Client that the Project Supervisor is and will continue to be a competent person to carry out its duties under this Deed and the Construction Regulations and has allocated and will allocate sufficient resources to enable itself to comply with the requirements and prohibitions imposed on the Project Supervisor by this Deed and under the relevant statutory provisions. In this Deed, **competent person** and **relevant statutory provisions** are construed according to section 2 of the Safety, Health and Welfare at Work Act 2005, and any amendment to it.

6. The Project Supervisor represents and warrants to the Client that the time allowed by the Contract for the completion of the Works is appropriate and sufficient to enable the Project Supervisor to perform its duties under this Deed and the Construction Regulations.

7. The Project Supervisor represents and warrants to the Client that the information provided by the Client to the Project Supervisor about the state or condition of the Site (as defined in the Contract) and any premises on it is appropriate and sufficient to enable the Project Supervisor to perform its duties under this Deed and the Construction Regulations.

8. The Project Supervisor shall ensure that it is insured by insurances in the same terms as the insurances the Contractor is required to have under clauses 3.6 and 3.7 of the Conditions of the Contract, and that those insurances comply with all the requirements of the Contract, and are kept in force for the same period as required by the Contract, and include cover for death or injury resulting from the Project Supervisor's performance or non-performance of its duties under this Deed and the Construction Regulations.

9.   If the Project Supervisor breaches its obligations or warranties under this Deed, or if the Contractor's duty to complete the Works is terminated under the Contract, the Client may terminate the Project Supervisor's appointment under this Deed.

10. Without limiting its obligations under the Construction Regulations, the Project Supervisor shall give the Client all documents it prepares in the course of and for the purpose of performing its duties under this Deed (**Project Supervisor's Documents**). If the Project Supervisor's appointment under this Deed terminates, the Project Supervisor shall give all Project Supervisor's Documents to the Client immediately. Ownership of and copyright in the Project Supervisor's Documents shall become the Client's when the Project Supervisor delivers them to the Client, or the appointment is terminated, whichever is earlier. The Project Supervisor shall indemnify the Client against any liability resulting from the use or copying of the Project Supervisor's Documents infringing the property (including intellectual property) rights of any person.

11. This Deed is governed by and construed according to Irish law. The parties submit to the jurisdiction of the Irish courts in relation to all matters concerning it.

Given under the Client's seal

Given under the Project Supervisor's common seal

MODEL FORM 11

FORM OF APPOINTMENT OF PROJECT SUPERVISOR FOR DESIGN PROCESS ONLY

THIS DEED is made on ....

BETWEEN

1. .... (the **Client**) and

2. ....
    whose registered office is at .... (the **Project Supervisor**)

BACKGROUND

By a contract (the **Contract**) made on or about (date of letter of acceptance), the Client, as employer, has appointed [...] as contractor (the **Contractor**), for [*insert name of Contract*] (the **Works**).

This Deed is collateral to the Contract.

IT IS AGREED AS FOLLOWS:

1. The Client appoints the Project Supervisor as project supervisor for the design process according to the Safety, Health and Welfare (Construction) Regulations 2006, and any amendment to them (the **Construction Regulations**) for the project comprising the Works [and – *specify any additional scope for which this Project Supervisor is to be appointed project supervisor for the design process, for example a process installation*] (the **Project**).

2. The Project Supervisor's appointment starts on the date of this Deed and continues for as long as, under the Construction Regulations, the Client is required to have a project supervisor for the design process for the Project, unless the appointment is terminated earlier.

3. The Project Supervisor accepts the appointment.

4. The Project Supervisor shall perform all of its duties under the Construction Regulations as project supervisor for the design process for the Project.

5. The Project Supervisor represents and warrants to the Client that the Project Supervisor is and will continue to be a competent person to carry out its duties under this Deed and the Construction Regulations and has allocated and will allocate sufficient resources to enable itself to comply with the requirements and prohibitions imposed on the Project Supervisor by this Deed and under the relevant statutory provisions. In this Deed, **competent person** and **relevant statutory provisions** are construed according to section 2 of the Safety, Health and Welfare at Work Act 2005, and any amendment to it.

6. The Project Supervisor represents and warrants to the Client that the time allowed by the Contract for the completion of the Works is appropriate and sufficient to enable the Project Supervisor to perform its duties under this Deed and the Construction Regulations.

7. The Project Supervisor represents and warrants to the Client that the information provided by the Client to the Project Supervisor about the state or condition of the Site (as defined in the Contract) and any premises on it is appropriate and sufficient to enable the Project Supervisor to perform its duties under this Deed and the Construction Regulations.

8. The Project Supervisor shall ensure that it is insured by insurances in the same terms as the insurances the Contractor is required to have under clauses 3.6 and 3.7 of the Conditions of the Contract, and that those insurances comply with all the requirements of the Contract, and are kept in force for the same period as required by the Contract, and include cover for death or injury resulting from the Project Supervisor's performance or non-performance of its duties under this Deed and the Construction Regulations.

9. If the Project Supervisor breaches its obligations or warranties under this Deed, or if the Contractor's duty to complete the Works is terminated under the Contract, the Client may terminate the Project Supervisor's appointment under this Deed.

10. Without limiting its obligations under the Construction Regulations, the Project Supervisor shall give the Client all documents it prepares in the course of and for the purpose of performing its duties under this Deed (Project Supervisor's Documents). If the Project Supervisor's appointment under this Deed terminates, the Project Supervisor shall give all Project Supervisor's Documents to the Client immediately. Ownership of and copyright in the Project Supervisor's Documents shall become the Client's when the Project Supervisor delivers them to the Client, or the appointment is terminated, whichever is earlier. The Project Supervisor shall indemnify the Client against any liability resulting from the use or copying of the Project Supervisor's Documents infringing the property (including intellectual property) rights of any person.

11. This Deed is governed by and construed according to Irish law. The parties submit to the jurisdiction of the Irish courts in relation to all matters concerning it.

Given under the Client's seal

Given under the Project Supervisor's common seal

MODEL FORM 12

FORM OF PROFESSIONAL INDEMNITY INSURANCE CERTIFICATE
(Clause 3.9.6)

[*Date*]

To [*Employer*]
Re [*Name of Contract*]

A Dhaoine Uaisle

We refer to the above Contract.

We are the insurance brokers/underwriter in relation to the Contractor's professional indemnity insurance. We confirm that the details of the Contractor's professional indemnity insurance set out below are true and accurate in all respects.

1. Insurance Company

2. Policy No.(s)

3. Retroactive Date(s)

4. Renewal Date(s)

5. Occupation as stated in the policy(ies)

6. Limit of Indemnity

    (a) Any One Claim   €

    (b) Any One Period   €

7. The insurance includes legal liability in respect of

    (a) death, bodily injury or disease to persons (other than employees):   YES/NO

    (b) damage to third party property: YES/NO

    resulting from breach of the Contractor's professional duties

8. (a) The insurance covers claims arising out of the sub-contracting of
         design or supervision activities, if any, to sub-contractors/sub-consultants: YES/NO

    (b) The adequacy of the professional indemnity insurances arranged by
         such sub-contractors/sub-consultants has been investigated and confirmed: YES/NO

9. The insurance includes:

    (a) Liability as project supervisor for:-

        (iii) design process: YES/NO

        (iv) construction stage: YES/NO

    (b) Liability under Collateral Warranties or Duty of Care Agreements: YES/NO

10. The insurance provides full policy cover in respect of:-

    (a) Date Recognition / Year 2000 problems: YES/NO

    (b) Pollution / contamination: YES/NO

    (c) Composite panels: YES/NO

    (d) Asbestos: YES/NO

11.   The amount of Policy Excess, if any, is: €

12.   (a)   Territorial Limits in relation to the insurance are:

      (b)   Jurisdiction is limited to:

13.   Restrictive endorsements/warranties on the policy:-
      ....
      ....

Is mise, le meas

Signed:

(Insurer & Insurance broker)

MODEL FORM 13

FORM OF COLLATERAL WARRANTY
(Clause 5.5)

THIS DEED is made on ....

BETWEEN

1. ....,
    whose registered office is at .... (the **Contractor**)

2. ....,
    whose registered office is at ....(the **Specialist**) and

3. [*Insert Employer's name*]..
    whose principal office is at [*insert*]..(the **Employer**).

BACKGROUND

A. The Employer has entered or is about to enter into a contract by which the Contractor will undertake to [name of the Contract] (the **Works**) on behalf of the Employer. Terms defined in that contact have the same meaning in this Deed.

B. By written agreement dated .... (the **Contract**) the Contractor has appointed the Specialist to (description of contract works or services or supply) in connection with the Works.

C. The total amount to be paid by the Contractor to the Specialist under the Contract for completing the Specialist's obligations under the Contract is €...

IT IS AGREED as follows in consideration of the payment of €1 by the Employer to the Specialist (receipt of which the Specialist acknowledges):

1. **Specialist's Undertakings to the Employer**

    1.1 The Specialist warrants and undertakes to the Employer that it has not broken and will not break any express or implied term of the Contract.

    1.2 The Specialist covenants with the Employer that, in carrying out the Contract, [the Specialist has exercised and will continue to exercise the standard of skill, care and diligence reasonably to be expected of properly qualified persons providing works, services or supply comparable in value, size, scope, complexity and quality to that required under the Contract]/[that the part of the Works to be undertaken by the Specialist, when complete, will be fit for its intended purpose as described in the Contract][5].

2. **Insurance**

    2.1 The Specialist shall maintain professional indemnity insurance in the amount of at least €..................... [[covering the Specialist's obligations under this Deed for each and every claim or series of claims arising from the same originating cause] if the Specialist is not a consultant, the following minimum level of professional indemnity insurance may be used €......................... [which may be an annual aggregate limit]] until a date no earlier than six years from the date Substantial Completion of the Works is certified under the Contract. The maximum excess shall be €.....................

---

[5] Delete appropriate option. Specialists should be required to covenant fitness for purpose when a works item they are to provide is to be fit for its intended purpose.

2.2   When it is reasonably requested to do so by the Employer, the Specialist shall produce for inspection satisfactory documentary evidence that its professional indemnity insurance is being maintained.

2.3   The Specialist shall immediately notify the Employer of any cancellation, non-renewal or material reduction in the insurance.

3.   Copyright

3.1   [Ownership of and copyright in all Contractor's Documents provided or produced by or on behalf of the Specialist will transfer to the Employer when the Employer receives them.[6]]

3.2   The copyright in all drawings, designs, reports, specifications, calculations and other similar documents and written information (including all information stored on any disk, computer or processing facility) obtained or provided by or on behalf of the Specialist in connection with the Works, [other than Contractor's Documents][7] (**Design Information**) will remain vested in the Specialist.

3.3   The Specialist grants to the Employer, and all those authorised by it, an irrevocable royalty free non-exclusive licence to copy and use Design Information and to reproduce the designs contained in them for any purpose related to the Works including, but without limitation, to construct, complete, maintain, extend, let, sell, promote, advertise, reinstate and repair the Works.

3.4   The Specialist will not be liable for any use by the Employer of the Contractor's Documents or Design Information for any purpose other than that for which the Specialist prepared and provided them.

3.5   The Specialist shall pay and indemnify the Employer against all royalties and other sums for the supply and use of any patented or copyrighted articles, processes, information or investigations required to perform its duties under the Contract.

3.6   The Specialist shall, on reasonable demand, produce to the Employer a copy of all the Contractor's Documents and Design Information.

3.7   The Specialist shall indemnify the Employer against losses, liability, damages, claims, proceedings and costs suffered or incurred by reason of the Specialist infringing or being held to have infringed any copyright or other intellectual property rights in any Contractor's Documents or Design Information.

4.   Assignment

The benefit of this Deed is assignable.

5.   Step In

5.1   The Employer has no authority under this Deed to issue any instruction to the Specialist in relation to the Specialist's duties under the Contract, unless and until the Employer has given notice under sub-clause 5.3 below.

5.2   The Specialist agrees that it will not, without first giving the Employer at least 28 days written notice, exercise any right of termination of the Contract, or treat the Contract as having been repudiated, or discontinue carrying out the Contract. The notice to the Employer must be accompanied by all of the information referred to in sub-clause 5.5 below. The Specialist's rights of termination (and the like) will cease if, within the 28 day period, the Employer gives notice to the Specialist under sub-clause 5.3 below.

5.3   The Specialist agrees that, if the Employer gives notice requiring the Specialist to accept the Employer's instructions to the exclusion of the Contractor, the Specialist will deal with and accept instructions solely from the Employer in substitution for the Contractor as if the Employer had appointed the Specialist originally on the terms of the Contract.

5.4   Only if the Employer gives notice under sub-clause 5.3 above, the Employer will become liable for payment of the amounts payable to the Specialist under the Contract (except for amounts due

---

[6] Include if required under the main contract (Schedule, part 1C).

[7] Only Include if assignment of copyright required.

for work for which the Employer has already paid the Contractor) and for performance of the Contractor's other obligations under the Contract, but the Employer's liability will not exceed the amounts particulars of which were given in the notice under sub-clause 5.2 above.

5.5   The Specialist and the Contractor shall, if so required by the Employer at any time, give the Employer a copy of the Contract, particulars of the amounts paid to the Specialist under the Contract, particulars of amounts due and unpaid to the Specialist, particulars of amounts remaining to be paid to the Specialist under the Contract but not yet due, and any information requested by the Employer that is relevant to these amounts.

5.6   If the Contractor's obligation to complete the Works is terminated under the contract between the Employer and the Contractor for the Works, and the Employer so requires, the Specialist shall enter into a contract with the Employer or a replacement contractor for the Specialist to complete its obligations under the Contract, in the same terms as the Contract with all necessary changes.

5.7   The Contractor releases the Specialist from any obligation to inquire about whether the Employer's rights under this clause have become exercisable, and from any liability to the Contractor for complying with this clause.

6.   **Notices**

Any notice to be given under this Deed must be in writing and will be considered given if delivered by hand or sent by prepaid registered post to the address of the relevant party at the top of this Deed, or at any other address the relevant party may specify by written notice to the other parties. A notice will be taken to have been received on the day of delivery if delivered by hand, or 48 hours later if sent by prepaid registered post.

7.   **Common Law Rights**

Nothing in this Deed limits the Employer's rights at law.

8.   **Law**

This Deed is governed by and construed according to Irish law. The parties submit to the jurisdiction of the Irish courts in relation to all matters concerning it.

9.   **Joint and Several Liability**

The obligations in this Deed of the persons comprising the Specialist are joint and several.

Given under the Contractor's common seal

....

....

Given under the Specialist's common seal

....

....

Signed on behalf of the Employer

by ....

in the presence of

....

MODEL FORM 14

FORM OF NOVATION AGREEMENT
(Clause 5.4)

THIS DEED is made on ....

BETWEEN

1. ....,
   whose registered office is at .... (the **Contractor**)

2. ....,
   whose registered office is at ....(the **Specialist**) and

3. [*Insert Employer's name*]...
   whose principal office is at [*Insert*]..(the **Employer**).

BACKGROUND

A. By written agreement dated [*insert*] (the Specialist Contract) the Employer has appointed the Specialist to [description of works, services or supply] in connection with [*name of main Contract*].

B. The Employer has appointed the Contractor to do Works, which include what the Specialist is to do under the Specialist Contract

C. The parties to this Deed have agreed to the novation of the Specialist Contract from the Employer and Specialist to the Contractor and Specialist.

IT IS AGREED as follows:

1. **Payment**

    The Specialist confirms that all money due under the Specialist Contract to the date of this Deed has been paid in full.

2. **Novation**

    The Specialist Contract is novated from the Employer and the Specialist to the Contractor and the Specialist.

3. **Affirmation of Subcontract**

    3.1. Subject to this Deed, the Specialist Contract remains in effect.

    3.2. The Specialist is bound, and considered always to have been bound, to perform the Specialist's obligations for the benefit of the Contractor, as if the Contractor were and always had been named as "the Employer" in the Specialist Contract in place of the Employer.

    3.3. Similarly, the Contractor is bound, and considered always to have been bound, to perform the Employer's obligations for the benefit of the Specialist as if the Contractor were and always had been named as "the Employer" in the Specialist Contract in place of the Employer.

4. **Warranty**

    The Specialist warrants to the Contractor that it has not breached any of its obligations under the Specialist Contract.

5. **Release from Obligations**

    5.1. The Specialist will no longer owe any obligation to the Employer under the Specialist Contract. This does not affect any collateral warranty between the Specialist and the Employer.

    5.2. Similarly, the Employer will no longer owe any obligation to the Specialist under the Specialist Contract.

6. **Law**

    This Deed is governed by and construed according to Irish law. The parties submit to the jurisdiction of the Irish courts in relation to all matters concerning it.

Given under the Employer's seal

Given under the Contractor's common seal

....

....

Given under the Specialist's common seal

....

....

MODEL FORM 15

FORM OF RATES OF PAY AND CONDITIONS OF EMPLOYMENT CERTIFICATE
certificate to be submitted with each interim statement under clause 11.1

[*Date*]

To [*Name of Employer*]

[*Name of Contract*]

(Period of interim statement):

A Dhaoine Uaisle

We refer to the above contract. Terms used in this letter that are defined in the Conditions of the Contract have the same meaning in this certificate.

The Contractor certifies that, in respect of the work to which the interim statement referred to above relates, clause 5.3 of the Contract has been observed by the Contractor and the employers of all work persons on the Site. This certification includes, but is not limited to, the following:

- the rates of pay and the conditions of employment (including in relation to pension contributions) of each work person comply with all applicable statutory provisions, and those rates and conditions have been no less favourable than those for the relevant category of work person in any employment agreements registered under the Industrial Relations Acts 1946 to 2004

- all wages and other money due to each work person have been paid in accordance with the Payment of Wages Act 1991 and have not been more than 1 month in arrears or unpaid

- payments due to be paid on behalf of each work person (including pension contributions, where applicable) have been paid

- all pension contributions and other amounts due to be paid on behalf of each work person, have been paid

- all deductions from payments to work persons required by law have been made and paid on, as required by Law

- in relation to the employment of work persons on the Site, the Safety, Health and Welfare at Work Act, 2005 and all employment law including the Employment Equality Act 1998, the Industrial Relations Acts 1946 to 2004, the National Minimum Wage Act 2000, regulations, codes of practices, legally binding determinations of the Labour Court and registered employment agreements under those Laws have been observed.

Is mise, le meas

Signed: ....
Contractor's Representative
[*Date*]

MODEL FORM 16

FORM OF BOND – UNFIXED WORKS ITEMS
(Clause 11.2)

Bond No..............................
BOND AMOUNT: €..

THIS BOND (the Bond) is made on ....

BETWEEN

1. ....,
   whose registered office is at .... (the **Contractor**)

2. ....,
   whose registered office is at ....(the **Surety**) and

3. [*Insert Employer's name*]..
   whose principal office is at [*insert*]..(the **Employer**).

BACKGROUND

A. The Contractor has been appointed by the Employer for [*name of contract*] (the Contract).

B. The Contractor has agreed to furnish this bond to the Employer as a condition of payment for certain offsite Works Items.

C. Terms defined in the Contract have the same meaning in this Bond.

IT IS AGREED AS FOLLOWS:

1. The Surety guarantees to the Employer that if the Contractor breaches the Contract or the Contractor's obligation to complete the Works is terminated under clause 12.1 of the Conditions the Surety will, subject to this Bond, pay all amounts for which the Contractor is liable under or as damages for breach of the Contract, as established under the Contract, taking into account all sums due to the Contractor under the Contract.

2. The maximum liability of the Surety under this Bond will not exceed €.................................. When the Employer's Representative notifies the Employer:

    2.1. that any of the off-site Works Items referred to in recital B above have been delivered to the Site and title in them vested in the Employer and

    2.2. the amount that the Contractor is entitled to be paid for that delivery and vesting under the Contract in the absence of this Bond

    the Surety's maximum liability will be reduced by the amount so notified.

3. No alteration in the Contract or in the extent or nature of the Works, and no allowance of time under the Contract, and no forbearance or forgiveness concerning the Contract by the Employer, will in any way release the Surety from liability under this Bond.

4. The Surety will be released from its liability under this Bond on certification of Substantial Completion of the Works, except in relation to any breach by the Contractor or termination that has occurred before that date, written notice (including particulars of the breach or termination) of which the Employer has given the Surety within 4 weeks after this expiry date.

5. The Contractor undertakes to the Surety to perform its obligations under the Contract. This undertaking does not limit any rights or remedies of the Employer or the Surety.

6. The Contractor must promptly, and the Employer may, provide to the Surety by registered or hand-delivered letter to the Surety's registered office given above or to the agent named in clause 12 below a copy of any notice that the Contractor gives to or receives from the Employer under clause 12 of the Conditions. Breach by the Contractor of this obligation or failure to give notice will not give any defence to a call on this Bond.

7. The decision of a court or arbitrator in a dispute between the Employer and the Contractor will be binding on the Surety as to all matters concerning a breach of the Contract, termination under the Contract, and the Contractor's liability.

8. If the Surety is called on to pay the Employer's loss following a termination under clause 12.1 of the Conditions, the Surety may suggest a completion contractor to the Employer, but the Employer has no obligation to accept the suggestion.

9. The Surety will not be liable under this Bond for a breach or termination caused solely and directly by war, invasion, act of foreign enemies, hostilities (whether war is declared or not), civil war, rebellion, revolution or military or usurped power.

10. The Employer may assign the benefit of this Bond, without the Surety's or the Contractor's consent, by giving written notice to the Surety.

11. This Bond is governed by and construed according to Irish law and the parties submit to the jurisdiction of the Irish courts to determine all matters concerning it.

12. [The Surety appoints .... of ....
    as its agent for service of legal proceedings. The Surety confirms that the named agent has been irrevocably appointed and the failure of the agent to notify the Surety of receipt of a document will not invalidate any proceedings or the service of the document.][8]

13. Money payable by the Surety under this Bond will be paid in euro in Ireland.

Given under the Contractor's common seal

Given under the Surety's common seal

Signed on behalf of the Employer

....
in the presence of

....

---

[8] An address in Ireland is required when the Surety does not have a registered office in Ireland.

MODEL FORM 17

FORM OF RETENTION BOND
(Clause 11.3)

[*Date*]

TO: [*Employer's name and address*]

.... (the **Contractor**) has entered into a contract dated .... (the **Contract**) with you for [*name of Contract*].

In consideration of you making payment to the Contractor of sums that would otherwise be retained by you under the Contract, WE, ... having our registered office at .... undertake to pay to you, without further proof or conditions and without deduction or set-off, any amount or amounts up to €................................... on receipt of your demand in writing.

Unless a demand has been made, our liability under this Bond will expire on [90 days after the end of the Defects Period].

Any demand must be in writing addressed to .... and must be accompanied by your declaration that:

- the Contractor has failed to perform its obligations under the Contract or

- the Contractor's obligation to complete the Works has been terminated under the Contract or

- any of the events listed in clause 12.1 of the conditions of the Contract have happened

You may make one or more drawings under this Bond.

No alteration in the Contract or in the extent or nature of the works to be done under it, and no allowance of time under the Contract, and no forbearance or forgiveness concerning the Contract by the Employer, will in any way release us from liability under this Bond

[We appoint .... of .... as our agent for the service of legal proceedings. We confirm that the named agent has been irrevocably appointed and the failure of the agent to notify us of receipt of a document will not invalidate any proceedings or the service of the document.]⁹

This Bond is governed by and construed according to Irish law and the parties submit to the jurisdiction of the Irish courts to determine all matters concerning it.

Given under our common seal:

---

⁹ An address in Ireland is required when the Surety does not have a registered office in Ireland.

MODEL FORM 18

FORM OF CONCILIATOR'S AGREEMENT
(Clause 13.1)

This agreement is made between

1. [*name*] (the **Employer**)

2. [*name*] whose registered office is at [*address*] (the **Contractor**) and

3. [*name*] of [*address*] (the **Conciliator**)

Whereas:

D. The Employer and Contractor have entered into a contract dated [*date*] (the **Contract**) for [*insert description of Works*].

E. The Contract provides for the appointment of a conciliator for the resolution of disputes.

NOW IT IS HEREBY AGREED as follows:

1. The Conciliator shall act in accordance with the terms of the Contract.

2. For all purposes related to this agreement the Employer's, Contractor's and Conciliator's addresses are as follows:

    2.1   The Employer   [   ]

    2.2   The Contractor   [   ]

    2.3   The Conciliator   [   ]

3. The Employer and the Contractor shall pay the Conciliator's fees [and expenses] as follows: [*set out agreed terms or refer to separate letter*].

4. As between themselves, the Contractor and the Employer shall each pay one half of amounts due to the Conciliator under this agreement. As between the Conciliator and the other parties, the Employer and the Contractor are jointly and severally liable to the Conciliator. If one party pays the other's share of an amount due to the Conciliator, that party is entitled to reimbursement from the other.

5. This agreement remains in effect for as long as the Conciliator continues to act in that capacity.

6. This agreement is governed by and construed in accordance with the laws of Ireland.

7. Any dispute or claim arising out of or in connection with this agreement shall be settled by arbitration in accordance with the arbitration rules referred to in the Contract, amended as required.

Signed for and on behalf of the Employer

_____

in the presence of

Signed for and on behalf of the Contractor

_____

in the presence of

Signed by the Conciliator

_____

in the presence of

MODEL FORM 19

FORM OF BOND – CONCILIATOR'S RECOMENDATION
(Clause 13.1)

[Date]

TO: [Name and address of beneficiary]

.... has entered into a contract dated .... (the **Contract**) with .... for [name of Contract]. A dispute has arisen under the Contract and the appointed conciliator has recommended that €.................................... (the **Award Amount**) be paid to ....

Clause 13.1.11 of the conditions of the Contract provides that if a conciliator recommends payment of money, the party concerned must pay the amount recommended if the other party first provides a bond. This is that bond.

In consideration of your paying the Award Amount to the [Contractor/Employer] WE, ...
.... having our registered office at ...., undertake to pay to you, without further proof or conditions and without deduction or set-off, any amount or amounts up to the Award Amount on receipt of your demand in writing.

Unless a demand has been made, our liability under this Bond will expire on the earlier of:

- when you confirm to us in writing that the dispute that was the subject of the adjudication has been finally determined by an arbitrator or court, which has finally determined that the [Contractor/Employer] is entitled to the Award Amount net of any amounts owed to you

- the date 550 days after the date of this Bond.

Any demand must be in writing addressed to .... and either:

- be accompanied by your declaration that as a result of the award of an arbitrator or decision of a court, the [Contractor/Employer] is not entitled to the Award Amount net of any amounts owed to you or

- be made more than 500 days after the date of this Bond.

You may make one or more drawings under this Bond.

This Bond will become operative on payment by you of the Award Amount.

We will not be released in any way or discharged by time, indulgence, waiver, alteration, release or compromise or any other circumstances that might operate as a release of a guarantor at law or in equity.

This Bond is governed by and construed according to Irish law and the parties submit to the jurisdiction of the Irish courts to determine all matters concerning it.

[We appoint .... of .... as our agent for the service of legal proceedings. We confirm that the named agent has been irrevocably appointed and the failure of the agent to notify us of receipt of a document will not invalidate any proceedings or the service of the document.][10]

Given under our common seal:

---

[10] An address in Ireland is required when the Surety does not have a registered office in Ireland.

SAMPLE LETTERS FROM CONTRACTORS TO THE EMPLOYER'S REPRESENTATIVE

Sample Letters from Contractors to the Employer's Representative

Specialists to be Novated to the Contractor

Project ....

Request for Tender Clarification Number ....

Please provide details of the work costs, attendances required and the daily delay costs for the following named specialists who are to be novated to the contractor

Specialist A
Specialist B

This information is required for incorporation in the tender and is required by ....

Yours etc

Utilities on Site

Project ....

Request for Tender Clarification Number ....

Please confirm details of the investigations undertaken to date to establish the existence of any utilities on site. Please also provide details of correspondence or communications with utility firms.

This information is required by ....

Yours etc

Ground Conditions

Project ....

Request for Tender Clarification Number ....

Please confirm full details of the site investigations to establish existing ground conditions on site, together with the findings of trial hole excavated on site and the locations of the trial holes.

This information is required by ....

Yours etc

Right of Ways, Wayleaves or Other Burdens

Project ....

Request for Tender Clarification Number ....

Please confirm that there are no rights of ways, wayleaves or other burdens on site.

This information is required by ....

Yours etc

Planned Developments in the Area

Project ....

Request for Tender Clarification Number ....

Please confirm details of any planned developments in the area that may effect the works during the construction stage.

This information is required by ....

Yours etc

Trespassers, Protesters and Others on the Site

Project ....

Request for Tender Clarification Number ....

Please confirm details of any Trespassers, Protestors or others on the site who have been in communication or have communications from the employer.

This information is required by ....

Yours etc

Sample Letters and Notices for Contractors Using Public Works Contracts for Building and Civil Engineering Works Designed by the Employer

1. The Public Works Contracts for both Building and Civil Engineering Works designed by the Employer have a common factor – they require notification in writing by Contractors to the Employer and/or the Employer's Representative.

2. Such notifications may be formal notice expressed to be a condition precedent to the Contractor's rights under the Contract. In other cases notification in writing is necessary to ensure communication between the Contractor and the Employer's Representative and for the proper and more efficient operation of the Contract conditions.

3. Under traditional contracts many situations have been encountered where the lack of a formal written has been pleaded against Contractors (and Subcontractors). This can have the effect of barring them from remedies to which they would otherwise be entitled or of making it more difficult for them to secure their full contractual entitlements. The new Public Works Contracts places more emphasis on formalities, written notices and maintaining records.

4. The following set of sample Letters and Notices are prepared for consideration by Contractors.

5. Traditionally contractors have been anxious to preserve good relations between their clients and their clients' consultants; commercially, this is as important as observing contractual formalities. The new Public Works Contracts require formalities to be observed. When submitting letters and notices, Contractors are only carrying out what is required of them under the Contracts.

Condition 1.3.2   Inconsistency between Terms

If either party becomes aware of any inconsistency between terms of the Contract it shall promptly inform the other party.

TO THE EMPLOYER'S REPRESENTATIVE

We have discovered an inconsistency between ....(give relevant details).

We request your instruction under Condition 4.4 on this matter.

Yours etc.

Condition 1.5   Performance Bond

The Performance Bond must be provided to the Employer before the starting date. The starting date means the date the Contractor proposes to start executing the Works, as notified by the contractor to the Employer's Representative under sub-clause 9.1.

TO THE EMPLOYER

Re: Performance Bond

We enclose herewith the Performance Bond as required by Condition 1.5 of the Contract.

Yours etc

Cc Employer's Representative.

Condition 1.6   Parent Company Guarantee

If required, the Contractor must provide a copy of the parent company guarantee to the Employer.

TO THE EMPLOYER

Re: Parent company guarantee

We enclose herewith the parent company guarantee as required by Condition 1.6 of the contract.

Yours etc

Cc Employer's Representative.

Condition 3.9   General requirements concerning insurances,

3.9.6 Within 10 working days of a request from the Employer, the Contractor must provide the Employer with evidence that insurances are in effect.

TO THE EMPLOYER

Re: Insurances

Pursuant to your request dated ....under Condition 3.9.6 of the Contract for Insurance Details we enclose herewith copies of the Contractor's Indemnity/Public Liability and Employer's Liability/Professional Indemnity/Other (*delete as appropriate*) insurance certificates for your retention.

Yours etc

Cc Employer's Representative.

In addition the Employer shall be informed of any reduction, cancellation, renewal or non-renewal of the insurance.

Condition 4.2   Contractor's Representative and Supervisor

Details of the proposed Contractor's Representative and Supervisor must be supplied to the Employer's Representative

TO THE EMPLOYER'S REPRESENTATIVE

Re: Contractor's Representative and Supervisor

In accordance with Condition 4.2.3 of the Contract we enclose details of the Contractor's Representative/Supervisor for your records. The Contractor's Representative/Supervisor named in the Works Proposal is no longer available to us.

Yours etc

Condition 4.5   Instructions

4.5.2   If the Employer's Representative gives an instruction and calls it a direction, but the contractor considers that it is a Change Order, the Contractor shall be entitled to give notice under sub-clause 10.3 and the issue determined under clause 10. In addition to the requirements of sub-clause 10.3, the Contractor must give this notice before starting to implement the instruction, otherwise it will be taken to be a direction.

TO THE EMPLOYER'S REPRESENTATIVE

Re: Employer's Representative Direction Number/reference xx

In accordance with sub-clause 4.5.2 of the Contract we give notice that we consider the above referenced Employer's Representative's direction to be a Change Order. We shall provide further details in accordance with sub-clause 10.3 in due course.

Yours etc

Condition 4.6   Works Proposals

4.6.2   if any Works Proposals do not comply with the Contract or the initial Works Requirements or are physically impossible to comply with, the Contractor shall propose a change to the Works Proposals as necessary.

TO THE EMPLOYER'S REPRESENTATIVE

Re: Proposal for a Change to the Works Proposal

In accordance with Condition 4.6.2 of the Contract we propose the following change(s) to the Works Proposal:

Details

[Note: There shall be no extension of time or adjustment to the Contract Sum for this.]

Condition 4.6.2 goes on to state: *If the Work Proposals need to be changed because of a change to the Works Requirements the Contractor shall propose a change. The contractor shall submit any change to the Works Proposals to the Employer's Representative.*

[This proposal comes under Item 1 of Section K of the Schedule and is a Delay Event and a Compensation Event].

Condition 4.7   Required Contractor Submissions

Unless the Works Requirements say that a different procedure is to apply, whenever the Contract requires that a document or proposed course of action be submitted to the Employer's representative, the following shall apply:

4.7.1   the Contractor shall give the document or a statement of the proposed action and all necessary supporting information to the Employer's Representative.

TO THE EMPLOYER'S REPRESENTATIVE

Re: Statement of Proposed Action

In accordance with Condition 4.7.1 of the Contract we submit the Statement of the proposed xxx Works together with all supporting information.

Yours etc

NOTE
- **Employer Representative may object.**
- **Employer's Representative may request further information.**
- **Employer's Representative may object after he has enough information.**
- **Contractor shall make a new submission to meet any objection given within the period (4.7.8).**
- **Contractor may have to submit new submissions as necessary to perform his duties under the Contract and submit a programme showing his actual and current planned progress (4.7.9).**

Condition 4.8   Value Engineering

The Contractor may provide the Employer's Representative with a value engineering proposal

TO THE EMPLOYER'S REPRESENTATIVE

Re: Value Engineering Proposal for [Details]

In accordance with Condition 4.8 of the Contract we enclose a Value Engineering Proposal for ....(details)

The proposal includes

(i)   Proposed changes to the Contract

(ii)   Proposed changes to the Contractor's Documents

(iii)   Detailed breakdown of the original cost for the relevant Work

(iv)   The projected cost of the proposal

(v)   The proposed adjustment to the Contract Sum to reflect the saving

(vi)   The proposed changes to the programme.

Condition 4.9   Programme

Before the starting date the Contractor must submit a programme to the Employer's Representative

TO THE EMPLOYER'S REPRESENTATIVE

Re: Construction Programme

In accordance with Condition 4.9.1 of the Contract we enclose the construction programme for the works for your information.

Yours etc

Condition 4.9   Programme

Before the starting date the Contractor must submit a programme to the Employer's Representative and the programme will identify dates when items are required from the Employer

TO THE EMPLOYER'S REPRESENTATIVE

Re: Dates of Information Required

i)   Please supply all the reinforcement schedules for the project by ....

ii) List all other items

Yours etc

Condition 4.17   Contractor's things not to be removed

TO THE EMPLOYER'S REPRESENTATIVE

Re: Removal of Items from Site

In accordance with Condition 4.17 of the Contract we advise you that we intend removing the followings from site .... on ....

Yours etc

Condition 5.4.1

...The contractor shall submit details to the Employer's Representative of any proposed specialist, other than one named in the Contract or when the Contract provides other procedures...

TO THE EMPLOYER'S REPRESENTATIVE

Re: Proposed Specialists for the ....Works

In accordance with Condition 5.4.1 of the Contract we submit details of proposed specialist xxxxx Limited for the supply and installation of the xxx works.

Yours etc

Condition 5.4.5

....the Contractor shall not terminate, allow to be terminated or accept a repudiation of such a Contract without first submitting details to the Employer's Representative, except...

TO THE EMPLOYER'S REPRESENTATIVE

In accordance with Condition 5.4.5 of the Contract we advise you of our intention to terminate the sub-contract with xxx Limited, the specialist appointed for the xxx works. The reason for the termination is ....

We propose to replace xxx Limited with xxx Limited.

Yours etc

Condition 7.8 Archaeological Objects and Human Remains

The contractor shall inform the Employer's Representative

TO THE EMPLOYER'S REPRESENTATIVE

Re: Archaeological Objects

In accordance with Condition 7.8 of the Contract we advise you of the discovery of .... on site. We have preserved the area concerned and await your instructions in this regard.

Yours etc

Condition 8.3.3 Inspection

The Contractor shall notify the Employer's Representative before any work item that is to be inspected is covered or packed.

TO THE EMPLOYER'S REPRESENTATIVE

In accordance with Condition 8.3.3 of the Contract we advise you that ......Works/Items are available for your inspection. The ....Works/Items will be covered on .... date.

Yours etc

Condition 9.1　Starting Date

TO THE EMPLOYER'S REPRESENTATIVE

Re: Starting Date

In accordance with Condition 9.1 of the Contract we advise you that we propose to commence works on ....(Date). This is the Starting Date under the Contract.

Yours etc

Requirements:　(i)　Minimum 15 working days' notice to the Employer's Representative

　　　　　　　　(ii)　Maximum 20 working days after the Letter of Acceptance

Condition 9.2.3　Suspension

If a suspension that is not caused by a Contractor's breach lasts more than three months the Contractor may request the Employer's Representative permission to proceed

TO THE EMPLOYER'S REPRESENTATIVE

Re: Suspended Works

Further to your instruction dated .... reference ...... to suspend the Works, in accordance with Condition 9.2.3 we request permission to proceed with the Works.

Yours etc

Condition 9.2.3(2)　Suspension

If the Employer's Representative does not give permission within 28 days after being requested to do so, the Contractor may, by giving notice to the Employer's Representative, terminate the Contractor's obligations under the Contract. In addition a notice would have to be submitted under Condition 12.4.2 and sent to the Employer.

Condition 9.3.1 Delay and Extension of Time

If the Contractor becomes aware that the Works is being or is likely to be delayed it shall as soon as practicable notify the Employer's Representative of the delay and its cause.

TO THE EMPLOYER'S REPRESENTATIVE

Re: Notice of Delay (Number 1, 2, 3, etc. – a log of Delay Notices should be maintained)

We hereby give notice under Condition 9.3.1 of the Contract that we have today become aware that the Works are being delayed /or are likely to be delayed by reason of (state cause). We also advise that we shall provide full details of the delay and its effect on the programme within 40 days of this notice.

Yours etc

Condition 9.6 Substantial Completion

The Contractor must request the Employer's Representative to certify Substantial Completion of the Works or part thereof.

TO THE EMPLOYER'S REPRESENTATIVE

Re: Request for Certificate of Substantial Completion

We hereby advise you that the Works (or section of the Works) will be substantially complete by .....(date). In accordance with Condition 9.6.2 of the Contract we request you to certify Substantial Completion on that date.

Yours etc

Condition 10.3   Contractor's Claims

If the Contractor considers that there should be an extension of time or an adjustment to the Contract Sum he shall provide such notice to the Employer's Representative within 20 working days after becoming aware (or 20 working days from when he should have been aware) of something that would give rise to an entitlement. The notice must prominently state that it is being given under sub-clause 10.3.

TO THE EMPLOYER'S REPRESENTATIVE

Re: Notice of Contractor's Claim(s) issued under Sub-Clause 10.3 of the Contract (Date and Reference).

In accordance with Sub-Clause 10.3 of the Contract we hereby give you notice of our claim(s) for an Extension of Time/an Adjustment to the Contract Sum/any Other Entitlement Under or in Relation to the Contract.

Yours etc

Within a further 20 working days the Contractor shall provide

TO THE EMPLOYER'S REPRESENTATIVE

Re: Contractor's Claim issued under Sub-Clause 10.3 of the Contract (Date and Reference)

Further to our Notice of Claim (Date and Reference) we enclose the following information in support of our claim:

  (i)   Details of all relevant facts;

 (ii)   A detailed calculation; and

(iii)   A proposal based on the calculation of the adjustment to be made to the Contract Sum;

(iv)   Details of the amount(s) of any other entitlement(s) claimed by the Contractor;

 (v)   Details of the effect on programme and completion dates

Yours etc

Condition 11.1   Interim Payment

TO THE EMPLOYER'S REPRESENTATIVE

Re: Interim Payment Statement Number (...)

In accordance with clause 11.1 we herewith submit our Statement for Interim Payment Number (...). We enclose the following details for your information:

- Statement showing the progress of the Works;

- The instalment that the Contractor should be paid;

- A detailed breakdown;

- Any supporting details the Employer's Representative requires;

- Certificate stating that the Contractor has complied in full with sub-clause 5.3 (Pay and Conditions of Employment).

Yours etc

Condition 12.3   Suspension by the Contractor

If the Employer fails to pay any amount due under a certificate issued by the Employer's Representative, the Contractor may make a written demand for payment

TO THE EMPLOYER

Re: Demand for Payment

We write to advise you that payment of the Employer's Representative Interim Payment Certificate number (...) was due for payment on ..... (date). This payment is now overdue. Unless payment is received within working 15 days of receipt by you of this demand we advise you that it is our intention to suspend the Works until payment is received.

This demand is issued in accordance with sub-clause 12.3 of the Contract.

Yours etc

If payment is not received within 15 working days from receipt of the demand for payment the Contractor, on giving notice, may suspend the Works until the amount has been paid.

TO THE EMPLOYER

Re: Notice to Suspend Works

Further to our Demand for Payment dated ...... we record that payment has still not been received. As a result we regret to advise you that it is our intention to forthwith suspend the Works until payment is received.

This notice is issued in accordance with sub-clause 12.3 of the Contract.

Yours etc

Condition 13   Disputes

TO THE EMPLOYER (REFER TO SECTION A, SCHEDULE, PART 1 FOR NAMES AND ADDRESSES)

We notify of a dispute under the Contract [details].

We advise you that this dispute is being referred to conciliation

This notice is given under sub-clause 13.1 of the Contract.

Yours etc

This notice is followed by a letter to comply with 13.1.2 for the agreement of a jointly appointed conciliator.

In the event of the parties failing to appoint a conciliator within 10 working days of the referral the conciliator shall be appointed by the appointing body or person named in the Schedule, Part 1N, on the application of either party.

Any dispute that can be referred to conciliation can be finally settled by arbitration provided the conciliator's recommendation is rejected by either party within the specified period.

INDEX